Mesry

From — All At Acntance

The Clydesdale Horse

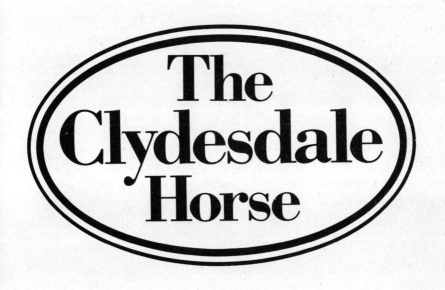

The Clydesdale Horse

Eric Baird

BT Batsford Ltd   London

By the same author:

Illustrated Guide to Riding

Horse Care

Horse Trials

© Eric Baird 1982
First published 1982
All rights reserved. No part of this publication
may be reproduced, in any form or by any means,
without permission from the Publisher
ISBN 0 7134 4041 4
Printed in Great Britain by
The Anchor Press Ltd.
Tiptree, Essex
for the publishers
B. T. Batsford Ltd.
4 Fitzhardinge Street
London W1H 0AH

Contents

Foreword

by His Grace
The Duke of Hamilton and Brandon
whose ancestor founded the Clydesdale horse

Much has been written about horses and breeds of horses, but Mr Eric Baird has now written *The Clydesdale Horse*, a definitive work on the history of and a tribute to that most famous breed which, sustained by careful selection by the early breeders, was given a sure foundation on which to build the future. This history records the parts played by former Dukes of Hamilton who, along with those other pioneers, could never have imagined the impact the breed would ultimately have as a power source on the land and in industry in many parts of the world until eventually displaced by the advent of the farm tractor. Nor could they have anticipated that the breed, even after this setback, could again increase in numbers as it became popular for show purposes in this country and in America and Canada.

Long may the breed flourish and the enthusiasm among the breeders continue so that future generations will have the pleasure of seeing this magnificent animal.

Lennoxlove
November 1981

Acknowledgments

The author takes this opportunity of acknowledging assistance and encouragement given by numerous individuals and organizations. Special tribute is paid to the painstaking reports of earlier generations of agricultural journalists – notably the great Archibald McNeilage – whose chronicles faithfully and proudly reported the progress of the Clydesdale horse around the world. Their work has been monitored through numerous volumes of *North British Agriculturist*, *Farming News* and *The Scottish Farmer*. Stewart Gilmour, former Secretary of the Clydesdale Horse Society of Great Britain and Ireland, was always most helpful, as was also his successor, my colleague John A. Fraser. Thanks also to Andrew and George Smith, W. Frazer Mellor, J. R. Raeside, Mrs Mary Gilchrist, Mr and Mrs A. Forsyth, Duncan Gillespie, Edward Hart, J. Douglas Charles of the Clydesdale Horse Association of Canada, Betty J. Groves, Clydesdale Breeders of the USA, Patrick O'Sheal of Canada, Hugh Ramsay, the staff of James Buchanan & Co. Ltd, and especially to Hugh McGregor, whose remarkable experience spans a long and important period of Clydesdale history. The late William Adair edited the Kilpatrick memoirs and was my mentor on this great breed. The Farmers' Club and Mitchell Libraries staffs were most helpful, and a host of people offered material and memories, whilst above all my wife, Janet, patiently tolerated masses of material spread around the home before it grew into a book.

List of Illustrations

Preface

To be able to introduce the Clydesdale horse and its breeders is a great privilege, because it is an important part of our heritage which must be remembered for past greatness and retained into the future. Anyone moving in farming circles will know that regard for the heavy horse is sincere, even in these more sophisticated times. Even so I confess that it was not until engaged in researching this book that I began to appreciate fully the extent of our indebtedness and the enormity of the contribution made to history and well-being.

Appreciation begins with understanding, so it seems likely that this work can help to show just why the horse is the object of much enthusiasm and pride, and the reasons why a good specimen still evokes passions akin to worship if not outright envy. But perhaps the most moving manifestation is the way in which succeeding generations continue quite naturally to absorb this Clydesdale lore, holding the trust in awe and venerating the mysticism. It is enough to say that there is still magic even in the very way in which a Clydesdale moves . . .

There have, of course, been dark periods, when we almost came close to losing the heavy horse; to the extent that there was serious talk of setting up a breed museum to preserve a few specimens and indeed the Clydesdale got on the Rare Breeds' Survival Trust protected list. Then like the Phoenix it rose again as a force – so much so that it looks set for multiplication the world over and demand has become phenomenal. Indeed there are those who maintain that the heavy horse may yet be restored as a principal source of energy for many operations, and where at one time such an idea seemed fanciful to the point of being scorned, few would be so hasty now as to dismiss the notion out of hand.

The heavy horse's major role in history resulted when it was the principal means of tractive power, on the farms and in city streets. It plodded through the hardest times yoked to those equine equivalents of the treadmill – the plough and the dray – and shared the labouring lot of mankind. At the same time the fashionable elite of stud representatives became elevated to a status beyond belief. As champions they were accorded the adulation and had the charisma which in modern times is the lot of star footballers or pop musicians. If you are sceptical of the claim, you have only to read on . . .

For the most part, however, it is the honesty and endurance, the character, of the heavy horse which leaves us in its debt, and it is seen rightly as a noble animal. There is, too, character in Clydesdale breeders, as rugged and determined as the giants they brought out. Their creative genius sprang from inherent knowledge, plus an uncanny and unerring eye for type and instinct for bloodlines and pedigrees. This owed nothing to today's sophisticated and computerized genetic studies and its source continues to fascinate scientists. Much the same sure touch and appreciation of type and line continue in the descendants of the master breeders, even if scope and use are admittedly more restricted.

It is right that we should revere the work of the founders of our livestock breeds. Men like Bakewell and Coates and those who fixed type were geniuses, and yet their achievements pale beside those who adopted a nondescript and variable cart-horse and turned it into an international force as work-horse of the world. It makes a marvellous story.

There are two features of the Clydesdale which it is necessary to appreciate and which command attention. The first is the wonderful action or springing step, covering a lot of ground in a straight forward movement. This active gait is the hallmark of the breeders' skills, and the most valuable attribute of the sound work horse. Secondly, and worthy of note, is the absolute perfection of turnout. All heavy horses do their grooms credit, but in the Clydesdale rings one sees excellence at all times: nothing less will satisfy. No horses are better shown; so fussed over to the point of absurdity. Showing is an act of homage and the means of creating both an impression and an image as well as a reflection of the innate skills of stockmanship with which is coupled the continuing quest for perfection. It is the summation of all that has gone into the making of the breed.

The Clydesdale has played a major role in the progress of agriculture and of industry, in north Britain and beyond it to almost every corner of the earth. It has been a major livestock export, in earlier years on a scale beyond credibility. Without doubt the full measure of its achievement was the way in which it helped to pioneer the opening-up of the vast American and Canadian prairie lands. When cropping nowadays calls upon such enormous power units we can only marvel at what was attempted and achieved by man and horse power in the beginning.

Lacking much of the glamour and wealthy patronage accorded the

English Shire horse, the Clydesdale should never have been thought the poor relation. It was not the progenitor, as some zealots would have it, but the Clydesdale and the Shire may have had a common ancestor from the Continent. The two breeds have certainly been inter-bred at various times, to mutual benefit, as will be seen from the story that follows. We can, however, be thankful that whilst they came close to merging their identities as cart horses, the irrevocable fatal step was never taken, and so they have remained near relations but altogether different types.

One may be forgiven for wondering whatever possessed the pioneers of the Clydesdale, moving them to pay fantastic sums, engage in costly lawsuits, and go to any lengths to gain possession of their chosen horses. They were as bloodstock tycoons, great personalities of their day, egotistical and idealistic beyond belief and seem now as peers among plain farmers. Still, if their horses were status symbols then it can be said that they were fantastically profitable, not to mention virile enough to be the sex symbols of the time. Their legendary prowess lives on!

A point to mention is that breeding this kind of stock is a lifetime's task, with son following father in the continuous pursuit of some type objective. From conception to maturity is all of a five-year term, if things go well, and nature can be a fickle partner in such enterprises. Stud work calls for deft and skilful manipulation of the genes, just as the artist perfects brush strokes, and much can go amiss amongst fecundity and management. Nor is there any sure means of measuring success – unlike, for example, racehorses which can be timed over the track, or cattle with a measurable output. It would take half a lifetime to prove the work output and economy of the draught horse, which was expected to operate singly or in the team, through all the hours of daylight on every day of the year, and often enough draw the family to church on Sundays too. Fitness was all. I have never once discovered any data on what amounted to a reasonable lifetime's work, or of horsepower in terms of, say, input of oats consumed. It was measured by intuition and one suspects horses were matched against the men of their time, so that they were bred to work without ceasing on as little as possible for as long as possible.

Perhaps now we do tend to look upon heavy horses more as ornaments, and as symbols of man's past experiences. But they are nevertheless still in use for work purposes; moreover they continue to prove that they can work the land when tractor power bogs down, and ecologically they live off and benefit the land in ways which would repay study. Hoofprints are less damaging to soil structure under some conditions than the ever-increasing compaction of tractor wheels and should there be less mechanical cultivation in the future then perhaps the horse will

become the most economical energy unit, mid-way between sophisticated, specialized machinery and all-out chemical based husbandry
systems which ignore cultivation by machine.

This book's purpose is to pay tribute to a heavy horse that has been
the backbone of food production, and the major source of transpor-
tation. It has been an influence for good over many generations through
a surprising diversity of activities, most of which continue. The Clydesdale is an honest, handsome and active equine, worthy of honour and a
place in history. With it we must link those who made and supported it;
besides, they entertained us and kept the wheels turning. I believe their
story is absorbing and will be appreciated by the widest readership.
Purists will complain that I would have done the job better by being
more meticulous about pedigrees and records, with due and detailed
recognition to all who played any part. I acknowledge the point of view
but 'tis better to tell an interesting tale in honour of the Clydesdale than
simply to keep the record for the few.

The Clydesdale Horse

Thudding hoof and flowing hair
Style and action sweet and fair
Bone and sinew well defined
Movement close, in front, behind.
Muscle strong, and frame well knit
Strength personified and fit.
Thus the Clydesdale – see him go
To the field, the stud, the show.

Noble eye, and handsome head,
Bold, intelligent, well-bred;
Lovely neck, and shoulder laid
See how shapely he is made.
Proper back, and rib well-sprung
Sound of limb, and sound of lung.
Powerful loin and quarter wide
Grace and majesty allied;
Basic horse, power-living force –
Equine King – The Clydesdale horse!

(with acknowledgment to O. R. Cadian,
North British Agriculturist, 1937)

One

Early History

Pride in the present-day Clydesdale horse is such that it becomes difficult to accept that it was not indigenous to the country, and its distinctive type was evolved by the natural skills of nineteenth-century stockbreeders. Accordingly the history can be traced back little more than 150 years. Nor is there much scope for romanticizing links with the so-called Great Horses of Europe, which stirred memories of the fifteenth and sixteenth centuries so vividly, when crowned heads were active in passing laws to favour the breeding of larger and more powerful horses and constantly making importations of stock to this end.

The Clyde horse was, in the beginning, in much the same position as the English Shire, with some common ancestry among the war horses that were brought in to upgrade native stock. The two types of cart horse were complementary, and certainly inter-bred to a considerable extent, even to the point when serious thought was given to merging them into one stud book. Fortunately it did not happen, and the two breeds went their separate ways to great advantage.

Before detailing the horses' antecedents it might be as well to set them in better perspective. We tend to take for granted that horses have always been a domesticated part of man's life, but such is not the case. Whilst the Egyptians put them to use as long ago as 1650 BC, the first known use for draught purposes in Britain was in East Anglia during the twelfth century, although it is accepted that the Bayeux tapestry gives a hint of this use too. It was not until musketry and cannon came into action for warfare that heavy horses were thought of in terms of farm work. On the land it was a case of oxen coming first, and up to the end of the eighteenth century these patient beasts prepared all the plough land, with as many as 12 yoked up two abreast. The last ten plough oxen in Britain were sold off the estate of Corse in the north only in 1826, and with regret because it was felt they had advantage over horses in being saleable for butcher meat. An old Welsh edict in fact prohibited the use of horses for ploughing in favour of oxen.

Horses really began replacing oxen in cart, and later in plough, very gradually from the sixteenth century and the reign of Elizabeth I, when horse breeding began to keep pace with increasing demand. Then in parts of Yorkshire and the Borders the breeding of horses and cattle became more important than that of sheep. A very good explanation for the slow succession of horses for work was because there were no suitable implements for them. As late as the eighteenth century in Scotland, creels or baskets were being used to carry manure out on to the fields. There were very few carts, and those in use must have been clumsy with wooden axles that moved along with the wheels, making them difficult to turn. Moreover dried rushes or twisted fir roots were used as harness traces, with hemp rope and iron chain scarcely known.

Even by the mid-eighteenth century there are reports of wooden implements scarcely scratching the surface of the ground. Horses were invariably used only with harrows, and even then were harnessed in teams of six. So there is little doubt but that they must have been lightweights; probably more like native ponies than draught animals. This is borne out by evidence that the plough was always followed by a man with a spade, to make the mould enough to cover the seed. A Galloway plough drawn by four horses, with a man to lead, was a novelty in 1644 and a survey made between 1773 and 1782 found plough teams ranging from 12 oxen yoked in pairs to four horses abreast, with every conceivable combination between these two extremes.

Improvements in tillage operations date from the mid-eighteenth century, which appears to coincide with wider use of horse-power, including better implements and improved character being bred into the draught horses. This is not to say that there were not heavy horses in existence. The earliest remains of such types have been dated back about 100,000 years, and Europe had good-sized types from earliest times but not domesticated or much resembling those we know. As type evolved it was more akin to the thick-set cob than any of great stature. This extreme of type can still be seen in various existing European breeds, many of which seem gross in proportion and as a result not great movers. All the evidence, particularly that extant in sketch form, points to the absence of big draught sorts; even the so-called Great Horse of medieval times is unlikely to have been the 17–18 hands high giant of dreams – although there was a size between that and a weight-carrying draught cob which could have served all purposes. This would have been useful for heavy cavalry, could carry armour, and at the same time move smartly over the ground. If there were indeed horses of colossal stature then they were none too plentiful, judging by the constant efforts made to foster their like.

In Britain and many other countries the sturdy native ponies, such as the Highland, Welsh, New Forest and Dales, were the most common, and hardy, stocky workers they were too. These were certainly used in pre-Roman times, and up to recently were much valued also for draught purposes. That such ponies became crossed with horses brought in by invaders is known, and there are many stories concerning ship-wrecked stallions being driven ashore and breeding with native mares. Judging by the descendants many must have been prepotent Arabians.

By the mid-eighteenth century then, the likeliest types to have contributed to a local heavy horse strain in Scotland and northern counties would be the Highland, the Flemish black horses which were regularly traded, and a variety of pack horses. There were also the Galloway nags, referred to by Shakespeare in Henry IV as 'a certain race of little horses in Scotland . . . lighter for hunting' and the Hollinshead Chronicles of 1577 made similar reference. An 1840 description of them is hardly flattering, as mostly of a dirty kind of brown, with little hair on the legs carried on top of the ankles like a heather broom. They had thin heads, long backs, and slatey ribs, and were also bad feeders. The Reverend Sam Smith's 'Survey' of 1810 regretted their decline, due to farmers breeding for weight and better adaption to draught. He mentions the Galloway as being 14–16 hands high.

Another keen observer of the countryside, Sir Walter Scott, noted in the novel *Fair Maid of Perth* that a gallant 'smith was mounted on a strong black horse of the Galloway breed, accompanied by a bonnet maker on a big Flemish mare with feet like frying pans'. The most likely forebears of the Clydesdale breed!

The Flemish horses are of special significance and we see their influence repeatedly. Lord Lovat is reported to have taken two of them up to the Highlands in 1810. Both were jet black, 17 hands high with big arched necks, well-feathered legs, big feet and good tempers. Many came over in Plantagenet times and King John was reputed to have brought in a hundred stallions which were much favoured by noblemen. That they helped to found the Clydesdale is certain, and it must be noted too that 'the great improver' Robert Bakewell used Flemish mares for a new generation of Dishley stock to found the modern race of Shire horses. They should not be confused with the Percheron, however, which was Breton or Norman in origin.

The pack horses which were mentioned have never been distinguished by breeding, but the suggestion is that they were lighter types of Cleveland, fore-runners of the Chapman pack horses, and by nature of their work might well have been inter-bred freely. Many differing types and strains travelled the newly made highways and there must have been regular out-crossings and infusions of strange blood. So-called improvement was often given official approval, as for example in James V of Scotland's Act of 1535, aimed at encouraging the improvement of native breeds of horse. As a result stock was brought over from Sweden and Northern Europe, mainly through contacts at the Scottish Court.

It was not always so, though, and successive English sovereigns up to and including Elizabeth I banned sales to Scotland and carefully controlled all horse-breeding activities, in order to conserve the stocks of the Great Horse type lost in the wars. Here is another pointer to the fact that only limited use of foreign bloodlines could be expected in the make-up of the Clydesdale, although to be sure it is highly unlikely that movement bans before the Union were ever really effective; indeed English black horses seem to have been prized plunder.

It is to the early reaches of Scotland's largest river that we turn to find the Clydesdale's natural home. It begins its 106 miles of meandering up in the hills of Lanarkshire, flowing on through richer market garden land in the Clyde valley. This is the area in which the special type of horse was bred, though it seems paradoxical now. In a later period the tentacles of the industrial revolution, epitomized by Robert Owen's New Lanark development for cotton spinning, displaced husbandry and gave the draught horse steady employment in the cities. In its way, however, the Clydesdale represented an even bigger revolution from this locality in the contribution it made as a source of energy or tractive power. And it out-lasted the loom.

The early recollections of the special type of Clyde horse being bred in Lanarkshire were that it stood smaller than is now accepted, but still heavier and more powerful than anything else then available; moreover it had a special aptitude for draught work. A springing, lively step was derived from the well-shaped pastern and extra large feet. It was said to be capable of drawing 20–30 cwt in a single cart, at a pace of 3½–5mph, and still be in a walking gait.

A parish statistical account dated 1792 stresses the excellence of the horse stock from the upper part of Lanarkshire brought to Rutherglen Fairs, stating that it reflected a high degree of credit on the farmers there for their unremitting endeavours to improve the stock. They were paying strict attention to every circumstance respecting colour, softness and hardness of hair, length of body, breast and shoulders, and it was said that no inducement whatever could lead them to encourage the breeding of a horse not possessed of the best qualities. Other reports suggest that all the colts brought to Lanark Fair in that period bore such distinct resemblance to each other that there was no doubt but that the district had distinctly superior draught horses, the results of careful crossing and judicious management. One noted dealer, Gibson from Bank of Pettinain, drove in 50–60 such colts.

According to legend the real origin of this improved stock was the result of a mid-to-late-seventeenth-century importation by one of the Dukes of Hamilton, a much travelled courtier, of six black Flanders coach horses. These were made readily available to local farmers for crossing with the common Scotch mares. In view of the general popularity of this type of Frisian strain this seems likely enough; certainly the 6th Duke of Hamilton (1742–1758) is recorded as having brought in a Flanders horse, dark brown in colour, for the use of tenants. Lord Lovat's pair of stallions imported in 1810 were described as Dutch or Flemish, and they were jet black in colour.

Mid-nineteenth-century writers appear to have had no doubts, for Dr Coventry and others stated that judicious crossing of the Scotch mare with Dutch stallions, with English Shire horses and with the heavy black breed produced the Clydesdale. Another authority confirmed the crossing of native mares with the Duke's Dutch stallion, stating that the bays and browns were prevailing colours, whilst the faults were a light body, overlong legs, and a hot temper at work. Andrew Henderson in 1826 wrote ' . . . that a pure enshapen possessed much of the appearance of the heavy black breed in cymettry [the Lincolnshire horse]. Stallions of that breed were much the rage in Lanarkshire some years ago. The present Clydesdale would appear to be a cross between heavy blacks and common Scotch mares.'

An interesting treatise on the Lanarkshire horse was written in 1815 by William Aitken, solicitor, who scotched the idea that Flemish stallions were involved. Unfortunately, however, he does not enlighten us further than to say that in about 1740 Robert Woodburn, tenant of Mains of Loudoun, sold what was then regarded as the best stallion in the area, at a price of five guineas. This underlines the stock improvement taking place systematically about that time, contrasting that price for a top animal with the £50 paid at Lanark Fair in 1815 for a 15-months colt, or £150 for a pair of two-year-old geldings in 1825.

Whilst these writers add something to the account, the most reliable source is Thomas Dykes, who in preparation for the founding of the Clydesdale Stud Book, of which he was the first secretary, made careful research of breeding lines by personal investigation and interview. He seems to have done the job most diligently, as a result of which much of the past was preserved for the record. So there is little dispute about the origins of improved horses, which have been traced to the family tree and records of the Patersons of Lochlyoch. According to them, some time between 1715 and 1720 John Paterson went to England and brought back a Flemish stallion, which was said to have greatly improved the breed and made the Upper Ward horses noted all over Scotland. Those Lochlyoch mares became famed during the late eighteenth and early nineteenth centuries. They were browns and blacks and had grey faces and some grey on the legs, with a spot or so on the belly which became recognized as a mark of distinct purity of breeding.

One might have expected that the place of origin was bound to give the name to the horses, marking their superiority, but this meets alternative propositions. Master breeder Lawrence Drew was fond of quoting an old groom to the Duke of Hamilton, who recalled that a horse called Clyde was introduced from the south to Lanarkshire, thus giving the breed its name. It could have been an outcross returned home! What is mostly accepted is that the name derived from breeders sending horses into the northern counties to travel, when they would be described as 'the Clydeman's horse' and later as Clydesdales.

Apart from Paterson stock there was report of a 16.1 hands-high stallion named Blaze, owned by a Scott of Brownhill and bought in Ayrshire about 1780 as a two-year-old. This was one of the first horses about which there was definite information. The horse was black and named Blaze from the grey mark on the face. No pedigree was known, but the sire was a Lincolnshire horse and the dam a local mare. It was said that he had a good share of coach-horse blood, leaving stock with a stylish shape and fine action. It is only fair to add that doubt was cast on this story, but Dykes was not dismayed and insisted his information came from Robert Weir of Brownhill, who had a good memory. Subsequent correspondence held that Blaze's dam was 'stolen into England and covered by a stallion there' being then recovered and producing a colt foal. A later owner, N. Scott of Liberton, seemingly showed the horse in 1784 to take first place or premium in an Edinburgh stallion show – the earliest awarded in Scotland for improvement of farm horses. He paid the high price of £21 for Blaze as a two-year-old, and kept him until he died aged 22 years.

A problem arising from the study of stock in early times is that owners were completely unimaginative when it came to names. As a result successful animals were perpetuated in endless and often totally unrelated stock. An old stallion bill, for example, dated 1807, refers to George Whyte of Brioch's 16 hands-high black horse Champion as being a grandson of the grey Old Blaze, but that is not to say that it was the same Blaze family. Taking the name was perhaps shrewd business tactics!

Useful foundation history was made in the purchase by Somerville of Lampits, nephew of Lochlyoch's tenant, of a two-year-old filly at Thomas Clarkson's sale in 1808. She became known as 'Lampits mare' and bred notable stock, including a stallion named Glancer (335) from which most of the good Clydesdales descended. A horse of some substance and weight, even if lacking the fringe of hair, he was foaled about 1810 when owned by James Thompson of Germiston, sold as a yearling to Alex. Kerr, Gallowberry, and then went back home. Ever afterwards he was known simply as 'Thompson's black horse' although he had grey hind legs and was faulted by the way for having too full a hock. The horse travelled at stud for a guinea, plus a shilling to the groom. A son was bred from him but he died early, so confusingly it is another Glancer II (337) out of 'Frame's Brown Bess' and possibly bred by Paterson of Greenhill, which is remembered and which won second prize at the first-ever Highland Show. It seems that as a colt this horse met with an accident, slipping between the planks of a bridge, so was ever afterwards 'Frame's lame horse' although indubitably sound for he got more mares in foal than any before him.

Another good foundation sire must have been R. Orr's Broomfield Champion (95) from Nethertown. Foaled in about 1831, the only produce of a grey mare, he won at the national show in 1834 and travelled widely before finishing up at Broomfield with the best of Frame's mares. Some said that he resembled Thompson's Glancer but this was later amended since he was a rich dark brown. The horse's dam may well have been the mother of Glancer II, but anyhow she was 'a goer' being ridden to market regularly by Frame who probably revelled in the way the regulars cleared a way to get a good look at her paces. Actually she appears from sketches to be more Cleveland than Shire, which might well account for the lively action.

Still there remains mystery surrounding that old grey mare, because Frame, as a leading stallion owner, was at some pains to follow a Highland Society directive that horses should be black, bay or brown bay, and he checked the tendency for greys which have been out of favour ever since.

What this does suggest is that even at this early date there was a conscious effort to breed to set type. Moreover as a result of the Glancer influence, enthusiam for claiming access to the fashionable blood became such that pedigrees began to be noted. By the 1860s there were a dozen 'Glancers' and even more 'Champions', and the pioneers worked hard to check them out for registration.

At around the same period that Thompson's Black Horse made a mark, John Brown of Kirkmuir brought out the best colt at the 1826 Highland Show, to win the premium with Sovereign (811) by Farmer's Fancy (297), son of Glancer. And one of the very first exports took place when Peter Crawford was paid the great sum of £160 for a colt which was presented by King George IV to the Grand Turk.

Closely linked with Frame as a pioneer is the name of William Fulton of Sproulston, who died in about 1850. A dealer, he travelled some good stallions. One of these was a son of Broomfield Champion, variously named 'Clyde' or 'Glancer' but more often as 'the ruptured horse' which again hardly impaired performance as his produce is now said to have made the Clydesdale breed. Bred near Lanark he was a small and unpromising foal but developed strongly. His son, named Clyde (155) and bred in 1840, was a winner. Some old stallion cards described him as 'Prince of Wales' which was anticipating events of four generations later for both parents of that famous horse trace back to the ruptured horse's line. The last recorded son, Joseph Barr's Prince Royal (647) from Muirhead, produced more winners than any contemporary, but was big to the point of coarseness.

The impression of early days is that Glancer stock was dominant, but they did not have it all their own way. That there were real differences in type is evident from Fulton's success and his comments that whilst 'Frame's kind have plenty of style and good action, Hugh Elder's have bigger and better bones and more hair'. Anyhow within 20 years the two were fairly well blended.

There were, incidentally, several specialized studs of grey mares at this period even if they were frowned upon in official quarters. Sir James Dalrymple Hay had a superior lot in Wigtownshire, which were related to the Clyde strains.

An example of how bloodlines were blended for success is shown in the work of Robert Anderson of Drumore. He bought a mare from Lampits that went back to the dam of Glancer, and amongst other foundation stock was a Brownsmuir mare which must have been a good one, for her foal Drumore Susie was unbeaten until 19 years old – and then by her daughter. She had 19 foals and helped to found the Victor line. Another purchase was a stallion named Old Farmer (576) by Blaze (74) and it is accepted that Anderson blended these lines to breed a distinctive and much favoured type. Results confirm this for his horse Salmon's Champion (737) was exported and his son, Lochfergus Champion (449), made a great impression on the breed. Fusion of Anderson's breeding strains produced Victor (892) with a temper 'like a lamb' and reputation for breeding famous mares. He went to Australia when seven years old. They did say the horse was 'rattle-skulled' but note that his son, Conqueror, bred the great Darnley.

Further evidence that other strains developed, based on Clyde's foundation, is seen from accounts such as those of Sir Charles Lockhart's Kintyre stock. Noting that the horses on his estates were little better than ponies, he took two improved stallions out, stipulating only that they were to be the very best and must be black, adding: 'The beggars don't understand anything that is not like their own cattle.' One tenant in fact secured a splendid colt from his best mare bred to the import, which went on to found a very superior race. Another success on the same peninsula was Farmer's Fancy (298) owned by John Erskine – this was another son of the ruptured horse, proving his prepotency as a sire on any type. He stood 17 hands high, drooped a bit about the neck, and had upright pasterns which affected the action. Not promising you might think, but that is the magic of stock-breeding. Progeny included a colt called Lofty (455) owned by Samuel Clark, and he bred a good mare of the Lockhart line, which in turn produced a top stallion in Sir Colin (772) which bred the famous mare London Maggie. There can be no doubt about the foundation influence of such stock. From this line in 1855 was bred Samson (741) that went to the renowned Keir stud and this superior horse, said to have given the breed its principal characteristics, bred Darling to be dam of the illustrious Prince of Wales (673).

Early records single out for praise stock from a horse called Old Stitcher (577), foaled before 1815 and of unknown ancestry but bred by Major Millar of Dalswinton. He must have been phenomenal judging by descriptions and was awarded a 40 guineas premium. Wilkin Brothers, Longtown, bred a son, Lofty (453) that was only ever beaten by his son, Young Clyde (949) said by judges to be the best cart horse in the three Kingdoms. Actually he was big ($17\frac{1}{2}$ hands high) and power-ful but poor sighted, and a dark bay with black legs. A handbill that was discovered claimed the horse possessed the full speed of the fleetest Arabian, with the solid strength of the dray horse. The mind boggles as to his exact breeding.

The Retrospective Stud Book of early registrations was somewhat confused with duplicate entries, including references to a popular sire line known as Clyde II (167), which was considered an outsider with coaching influence from Cumberland. He bred Briton (154), a leader at the Highland Show 1842, out of a winning Glancer mare. Keir Clyde (156) came off this stock in 1847 to found Sir William Stirling-Maxwell's stud.

A strain known as 'The Banffshire Comets' was fashionable and sounds fleet. It went back to 'Culleys brown horse' (571) out of Upper Ward. The first true Comet (191) was foaled in 1836 and went north to Robert Wilson, Portsoy, breeding good black horses and a dapple grey Comet (192) which was widely shown. He was said to have girthed $8\frac{1}{2}$ft in good condition, stood 16 hands high on short legs, and was well sprung about the ribs.

A new era in Clydesdale breeding came with a line founded by Sir Walter Scott (797) and was traced back to Old Clyde. The whole family became confused with George Scott breeding Scotsman (574) of unknown origin, made worse by his insistence that the mare was covered twice by different horses and both were unknown. Anyhow the descendant Sir Walter Scott was sent south to travel and would certainly have been used on Shire stock, so no doubt many of the produce would find their way north as improved horses. This much is confirmed by leading dealer, David Riddell, 'discovering' the stallion after several seasons and bringing him back.

One fact which does emerge is that there were fewer stallions or entire horses in those early days than might have been supposed, considering that they were worked constantly in the fields. It was seemingly not unusual for ploughing to be halted whilst the horse was loosed from the yoke or hitch to serve a mare. This is how the traditional groom's fee arose; to compensate for the trouble caused. A stallion was often kept between 20 or more farmers, representing 80 mares.

Reading the accounts of individual outstanding bloodlines one might question why improvement efforts were not co-ordinated. The Highland Society was formed in 1784 to improve agriculture and directly stimulated the development of horse breeding with the award of premiums from 1796 on, based on competitive appearance and produce. The idea spread. In 1823 the Society divided premiums into two classes with ten guineas for the best Clydesdale or other mare for working strong lands, and a similar award for the best Cleveland or other suited to draught on lighter lands. It was said the distinction arose from an article in the *Farmers' Magazine* of 1823, which urged readers to obtain a race of stronger and more active horses, pointing out that the difference in work output meant that out of five pairs of ordinary horses one pair might become unnecessary.

Only the home of the draught Clydesdale had the superior type, and for the stiffest land it seemed there could not be a better model, especially if proportioned in size to the strength of the ground. Apparently there was no great gain in body size as such, or for that matter in weight either, between the years 1826 and 1860. Yet it was the most significant time for the establishment of the breed, when its endurance and freshness of limbs was highlighted. A report from Montreal of horses seen in 1830 called them 'celebrated' for agricultural use, noting actually that they were also adaptable for saddle or as carriage horses.

As all too often happens in livestock breeding however, by 1882 it was said that a fine head had given way to one rather large if not heavy in proportion, while length of leg had given way to remarkably short, strong and hairy legs and compactness. Type features had become somewhat exaggerated.

As a final note it is worth recording the report of a horse show in the Bristol area in the early days, claiming that a Clydesdale stallion exhibited by the then Duke of Beaufort weighed nearly a ton but out-trotted all the hacks there in the course of a few hundred yards. That confirms the fleetness of foot and impressive action, which has always been the hallmark of a remarkable heavy horse. It was this character-istic which distinguished the breed from earliest times.

Two

Character Builders

The really formative time for the Clydesdale horse came in the mid-nineteenth century, when improved strains emerged to coincide with the general expansion of trade. The first great international heavy horse show was held in London and attended by royalty, an export trade developed, and with it a period of boom. It was in such circumstances that great studs were founded, when champion horses and their master breeders became surrounded with the aura of magic, and of money, which gave them star quality and assured a place in history.

People are the backbone of any industry, and this has always been true of stock-breeding; certainly there were men of character behind these giant horses. In the case of the Clydesdale two in particular had great influence in introducing the breed to the world, having an eye and skills for their art which were matched by native shrewdness and a knack for exploiting every opportunity.

One of these legendary figures was Lawrence Drew, born in 1826 on his father's farm of Carmyle near Glasgow. As soon as he became of age he was put into Merryton, a farm on the Duke of Hamilton's estate, and 15 years later became land steward – a post of some influence then. That he should turn his attention to the breeding stud of draught horses was no accident, because it was a necessity for the tenants to have good work stock; besides, being linked with the family which had, however unwittingly, helped found an improved strain of Clydesdales, it was natural that the reputation be enhanced if possible.

The other kindred spirit was a dealer, Davie Riddell, who was brought up at Park near Lenzie, began work as a callow youth and by the time he was 20 had become tenant of Kilbowie and soon of several other farms too. The two men became close friends. Both were characters and Riddell, in later life, was a majestic figure with rubicund features, feared and respected because he could influence a horse trade just by his presence. And besides, he had a voice like a clarion and a habit of making himself heard. The fact that he held a substantial contract for paving Glasgow streets made him a power to reckon with, as witness this boast: 'It takes me two days to see my horses. I have a lot here at Blackhall, more at Mavisbank, another lot at Kilbowie, and there's more among farms around, and then about a hundred standing in our city stables.'

Riddell won first prize in a national stallion show in 1858, with Champion (126), by Old Clyde, and in fact carried off seven championships and 31 first prizes. From then on he exhibited regularly and usually won. More significantly, however, it was this dealer that turned out the ancestors of the great sires of the breed in Darnley and Prince of Wales, which had such influence that he could be said to have laid the very foundations of commercial success. He brought out the stallion Sir Walter Scott, sire of The General (322) that bred Prince of Wales, and also Old Clyde (574), the father of them all, even if their antecedents were shrouded in mystery.

Cronies in every degree, Riddell and Drew influenced horse improvement but also attempted to wreck it by divisive tactics; simply because it did not suit them to record pedigrees scrupulously. A good example of their joint skills was seen when the London international show was held at Battersea in 1826, when both the Duke of Hamilton and Sir William Stirling-Maxwell of Keir were equally determined to win. Riddell scoured the country and discovered the stallion Sir Walter Scott in Fylde, Lancashire, selling him to Drew for the Duke's stud at the princely sum of £1,000. In due course he was male champion. But there were said to be only two mares in the country capable of winning and the dealer was given the task of selection between William Park's Maggie by Lord Raglan (492), off the same Old Clyde strain that bred Sir Walter, and the other contender similarly bred but owned by the Misses Stevenson of Bellahouston. Riddell preferred the first and when the two mares met in the show ring his choice was confirmed, and the crown went to the Duke's celebrated London Maggie with Keir stud reserve. So it was a great triumph for Drew, the Duke, and their canny dealer friend who fairly basked in the glory of it all.

When the 11th Duke of Hamilton died the following year, and his son being uninterested in continuing with the horses, a dispersal sale took place. Drew set up on his own account, taking the champion male and female horses along with others – including Old Rosie, known to be the progeny of a cart horse. It was that type of breeding which attracted him, which is why in due course he frequently introduced alien strains. His theory was that Shire and Clydesdale were but two divisions of the same, with characteristic differences attributed to environment and similar factors. In fact, though, he hoped the use of selected lines could establish a distinctive type of draught horse, and to this end travelled widely over Lincolnshire and Derbyshire especially, to seek out the mares he favoured. An enthusiast of the times, W. R. Trotter, stated that Drew drove for weeks at a time around those areas searching for stock, often in company with Saul Wade of Mickleover whom he would collect at 4 am off the night train. Many purchases were by the famous sire Lincolnshire Lad, also known as 'K' or 'Honest Tom', and on occasion he sold a whole train load of horses to his friend Hugh Crawford.

Both Drew and Riddell seemed to perpetuate an air of mystery about the horses they bred and handled, although there could scarcely have been much secret about their background. For example a Shire sired the mare Queen that won honours in 1882–3, and there was one called Netty which Drew insisted had been through so many dealers' hands he knew nothing about her. She went to Keir for the high price of 595gns and won the Highland Show in 1887. Curiously, following that success, the show directors selected that horse to have a portrait painted – she was seen to be the most perfect specimen of the Clydesdale breed at that time. This points to both type being markedly special and officials asking no questions about purity. Of course times were different: a Shire named Sheba was in the hundred-strong stud and took the championship for best agricultural horse at the Liverpool Royal, and was adjudged first prize Clydesdale at the Highland Show of 1878.

Whether Merryton stud would have made much impact in history had it not been for breeding the great stallion Prince of Wales is open to speculation. It was curious how this came about, as a result of Drew having to submit accounts for the farm following the Duke's death. The estate trustees objected to the high values he had put on some of the horses and he was asked for proof. To get it he sold two of them to his friend J. Nicol Fleming, who had leased the farm of Drumburle and was seeking stock. He chose a three-year-old filly, Darling, and also a yearling colt, Ivanhoe (398), classically bred by Sir Walter Scott and off London Maggie, paying £130 and £100 respectively. Now Darling was covered by Riddell's horse General, a son of Sir Walter, and the mating bred Prince of Wales. Nor is that the end of the story, for this foal, destined to be the greatest Clydesdale in history, was sold at three years old to Riddell and in 1871 an Australian breeder attempted to buy him. Drew remarked on the fact to his brother Robert, who was staying at Merryton after making a fortune in the gold rush. On learning that his brother believed this to be the best-ever horse he went out without saying a word and bought it. Riddell was said to have priced it as if to a stranger and been astonished when it led to a deal. The price has been put at £1,600 but could have been £1,250; either way it was sensational for the time.

The Royal family took an interest in Drew's stud, and in 1877 at one of the regular draught sales a two-year-old colt was bought for Queen Victoria at 400gns, as well as a yearling at 200gns which won the following Royal Show. In 1878 whilst staying at Hamilton Palace, HRH the Prince of Wales visited Merryton and was suitably impressed with his equine namesake, which seemingly moved as briskly as an American trotting horse. With the party were the young Prince Imperial and the Dukes of Hamilton and Manchester, and they saw 133 horses that day. His Royal Highness was said to have been vastly amused that the stud's most able groom was a woman, and that many of the mares were led out by girls, it being explained that they helped to make the stock more tractable. Drew had evidently gone to some pains to impress, building a very fine archway at the entrance gates, surmounted by a statue of his famous stud horse. When he wished to present a horse to the Prince as a memento of his visit the gift was graciously accepted, with selection left to the owner. It must have been a sound choice too, for the colt won the next Royal Show. On leaving HRH shrewdly observed: 'They are a grand lot of mares Mr Drew, but mostly Shires I think.' Merryton's response was equally revealing: 'All the better for that, your Royal Highness' he declared.

The famous stallion's reputation was steadily enhanced by the stock he bred, and the stud's fame grew apace. At the 1878 sale, for example, the horse's box was besieged by the crowd, whilst there was general agreement that the best two mares were the Prince's dam, Darling, and Darnley's dam, Peggy at Keir, although this was probably with hind-sight. Even at this time, however, Lawrence Drew's reticence over pedigrees was beginning to be watched closely; indeed to the extent that trade was affected. The catalogues began to carry sketches of the horses on offer, in an attempt to cover the deficiency. But faithful to his friend as ever, the top bids were invariably made by Davie Riddell.

In his own defence Drew frequently stated his views vehemently on pedigrees and registration: 'There is no man more interested in pedi-grees than I,' he would say, adding that English mares were the best for breeding with Scotch horses, and the good English mares ran from Scotch stock. 'There is no such thing as a pure Clydesdale, and I never in my life misrepresented a pedigree of an animal sold.'

That simple exposition of breeding policy was in fact most revealing, in that it showed a careful selection process and practice of hybrid-ization which many since have applied in scientific fields similarly to benefit the world. Many years later an eminent geneticist, A. D. Buchanan-Smith (later Lord Balerno) was to comment that the trouble was that Drew's hybrids did not reproduce truly. His analyses of the unofficial register, the 'Select Clydesdale Stud Book' as it was called, suggested that its protagonists were unable to see beyond the excellence of the first cross families, and were unappreciative of the value of the progeny test. They would not be alone in that failing.

It has been argued that Drew failed in his attempt to establish a particularly distinctive type, due to his early death in 1884, but can there be doubt that he laid the foundations for the modern Clydesdale?

Dispersal of the Merryton stud was a major event, drawing a crowd of 6,000 people, although interestingly enough they had a marked reluctance to bid. Faithful as ever Riddell helped to boost the average up to £152.2s.8d. for 63 head, taking amongst his many purchases the 19-year-old Prince of Wales for 900gns. Art enthusiasts might care to note that Nicol Fleming had had the horse painted by the Royal Academician Lutyens in 1869 when three years old, and the artist did a later portrait which was subsequently bought by J. M. Martin and became a possession of the Clydesdale Horse Society. Drew was given a replica, which was passed on to his brother Robert, and later sold for £120.

Whilst there is no doubt as to the influence and impact Drew and Riddell had on the Clydesdale's fortunes, the comment once made by John Clay, a stud book founder and American cattle rancher, is worth quoting. Recalling that Davie Riddell once remarked that Lawrie Drew and he knew more about pedigree than all Scotland together, and were going to keep that knowledge to themselves, Clay added: 'Their memories suddenly became defective on dams, but the sire was usually Prince of Wales. Drew over-played the game; perhaps because Davie Riddell's influence warped his judgement . . ..'

There might be truth behind this remark; certainly insofar as export trading was concerned. But still Riddell held an ace in the famous stallion Darnley, bred at Keir by Conqueror (199) with the Samson mare Peggy as dam. She was said to be as near perfection as any Clydesdale ever, and so influential that the experts were at pains to stress her purity. Darnley's value is seen in any breeding line, and his supremacy supported by the fact that at 12 years old he took the Edinburgh centenary show championship of 1884, and was then standing in Stranraer district at the record premium of £1,000. What had emerged as fact was that the most superior breeding line of all, or in stockmen's terms the best 'nick', was in stock by Darnley out of the Prince's mares.

In fact a debt is owed to Riddell by the heavy horse world, because he certainly helped to make the Clydesdale famous in America, Australia, and all over the continent of Europe; indeed wherever a stylish and powerful horse was in request. The very scale of his dealings enabled him to meet any order promptly; nor does there appear to have been serious dissatisfaction with any of the stock he shipped – unlike that of his successors at the business. That he spread the influence of good horses is seen from the sale of Chancellor (143) to Robert Wilkin of Christchurch, New Zealand, after the horse had had a season on a £400 premium to the Duke of Bedford's tenants at Woburn. His silver medal horse Time o' Day (875) went to Melbourne in 1875 for 1,500gns. In 1885 E. Bennett and Sons of Kansas, USA, bought 36 stallions and six mares from Blackhall, and this was described as the largest-ever sale from one stud to single buyers. Riddell would often point out to visitors the great stallions whose portraits covered the walls of his room, exclaiming with pride: 'I keep them in this country for to do the country good.' He was a bold bidder too, on at least one occasion taking 40 fillies from Waltham Fair 'as bonnie as were ever seen'. It was remarked that it took a long spoon to sup with Riddell & Co., but he was nevertheless regarded as trustworthy and never ran an opponent's horses down. A story to savour is his response to one who had the temerity to question his horse General's soundness of wind – back boomed the great voice that General was a roarer and his sire Sir Walter was the same. Then he added in a final riposte: 'General is the roaring son of a roaring sire, and there are roaring sons of roaring sires in human families too!' A rebuff calculated to silence any doubters.

Riddell was an anti-establishment figure, along with his friend Drew, and involved in any breakaway activities, as for example in 1876 when a rival event to the major stallion show was mooted. He promptly entered 18 horses, estimated as being worth all of £10,000 then and described as a show in themselves and virtually guaranteeing the event. He took the senior premium with Roving Boy, the junior gold medal with Luck's All and then refused £1,000 for the animal.

In those days horse dealers were not infrequently involved in court litigation and, in view of the scale of operation, it was not surprising that Davie Riddell had brushes with the law. One action which he raised was in 1879, in protest against the suggestion that he was insolvent. The great voice was heard to declare then that he was in fact wealthy, claiming estates and means to the value of some £60,000. His lease of Blackhall was from Sir Michael Shaw Stewart, a keen Clydesdale breeder, council member and leading land-owner. Because of the differences over registration there was speculation that he would not renew Riddell's lease; in fact he did so and moreover in view of farming's decline charged 25 per cent less rent. Apparently that surprised even the illustrious tenant.

After dominating the breed for some 40 years, Riddell's influence declined steadily following Drew's death. It was said that 'he resigned his premiership of stud horses' on the death of Prince of Wales. In truth, though, events overtook him and later trends in type meant that he was no longer at home in the showyards. Still, he never missed the big exhibitions and indeed in 1895, although ill, he like others before and since, attended the annual stallion show and caught a near-fatal chill. Recovering from pneumonia he lived to July 1911 and died at 83 years of age.

Riddell was honoured twice in his lifetime by fellow breeders, in 1891 and 1908. On the first occasion he was given a dinner service in solid silver and his wife a piece of jewellery; at the later event a fine portrait in oils was done by Fiddes Watt. The account of his sitting for this artist is amusing, particularly when he commanded: 'Now artist, let's get on with it' – his only remark to the artist in the whole sitting. Watt observed wryly: 'I painted him in the barn loft, amongst the animals he loved, so that he was at hand to direct the farm work and when wanted they called up to him. To give any order he simply cried out . . . and everyone heard.' The chairman at the presentation dinner confessed that he would not have been surprised to learn that Davie had subsequently sub-let the barn as an artist's studio. He was that sort of man. It should be added that at that time there were those (including Davie Riddell) who had a peerage in mind for him.

Dispersal of the stock at the dealer's death was an anti-climax, particularly as in the month of August there was a gale. Many of the horses did not reach reserves set and the top bid was a paltry 76gns for Crown Derby by Baron's Pride. Overall, 47 horses averaged only £44. It would have grieved the late owner, whose will showed estate of £15,700.

That two men should have exercised great influence on the Clydesdale breed in such unusual ways is remarkable, but proof too that they were owners of dominant and outstanding sires. Their success could be measured also in the active way in which they promoted these horses, but still we cannot overlook the undoubted introduction of new bloodlines on the female side and the influence they had on type. In the following chapter, however, we see how their fellow breeders were striving equally hard, in more orthodox fashion, by strict and legitimate registration of pedigrees and identification of the superior stock. Breeding heavy horses was to become both art and science.

Flashwood, foaled
1883

Prince of Albion

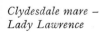

Clydesdale mare –
Lady Lawrence

Bonnie Buchlyvie, sold in 1915 for £5,000

Doura Majestic,
Cawdor Cup
winner for J. W.
Young and Son
in 1972

Spatted and part plaited, ready for show

Hugh McGregor and his team at work – note the way the hair stands out above the hoof

Above: A 850 gns-mare in 1952 – Bridgebank Dorothea

Below: Balgreen Final Command, an outstanding stallion and winner in 1944

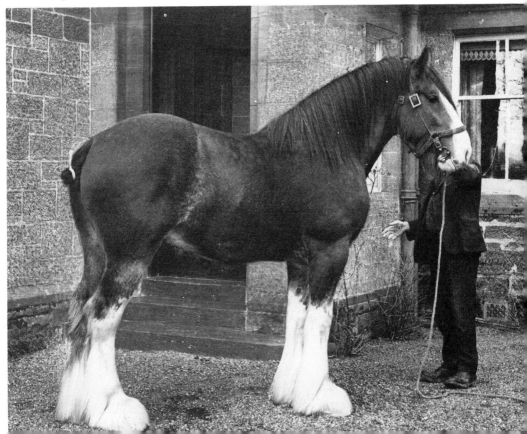

Above: Craigie Gallant Hero – the last of a great line

Below: Mr James Picken of the famous Torrs Stud judging at the Royal Melbourne Show. Mr W. B. Mahncke (right) showed the winning stallion

*Left:
Clydesdales
leading the
parade of the
Royal Show
of Victoria
stock past
Melbourne
Town Hall in
1978*

*Above:
Clydesdales on
their native
heath – a sight to
gladden the hearts
of all enthusiasts*

*Left: Forestry
operations, 1920*

Above: Early ploughing scene, Aberdeenshire

Below: A Clydesdale team at the plough – note the distinctive harness and characteristic bold stride

Three

Opening the Book

Whatever the progress made in any breed of livestock, it cannot be said to have been truly organized until a system of registration is set up and pedigrees are legitimized. That the National Stallion Show should have been staged 17 years before a Clydesdale Stud Book Society was formed is probably surprising to a generation who would now set the system before the stock, but in fact breed organization was born of the need to control the excesses of enthusiasm on the part of founders such as Drew and Riddell, and to straighten out differences with overseas buyers.

Back in 1876 there was a considerable trade in Clydesdale horses, and also rumblings of discontent regarding the making up of 'fancy pedigrees' and taking prizes with horses which then sold readily to Continental and Australian buyers, often with totally fictitious prices being mentioned. A committee set up to examine the feasibility of establishing a Stud Book found much evidence to support the need. There was, for example, a first-prize winner at the Highland Show for which neither the breeder nor the sire was known. And numerous winners of the time were named 'Prince of Wales'. The committee was assured that when buying a Clydesdale one generally gained a pedigree as long as the arm which was useless. A two-year-old might first be shown with pedigree unknown, then if successful in the ring would six months later prove to have become an aristocrat of noble lineage. It was considered that the tactics of certain breeders and owners were such as to engender grave suspicion, and that if allowed to go unchecked they might render the breed as proverbially discreditable as horse-racing. One good example was of a colt which won a prize without benefit of pedigree and then appeared as 'King of the Princes' by Prince of Wales and from a mare that was sister to Drew's chestnut mare. This was hardly a pedigree, even supposing the breeder really was 'said to be Peter Brown, neighbour to Davie Riddell' and it was often stressed that the latter made so many block entries for shows and sales that it was impossible for details to be given. That may well have been true. Yet the worst indictment came from Colonel D. R. Williamson, suggesting that a Stud Book could be the means of halting the improvement of what was called 'the Clydesdale horse' as its blood did not entirely belong to Scotland.

The meeting that was arranged to establish the Stud Book, and with it of course the breed society, was held on 26 February 1877, on the eve of the annual stallion show. The chairman was John M. Martin of Cardross, and there were 24 others present, which must have been disappointing in view of the enthusiasm usually shown in such matters. The Earl of Dunmore was there from London, and duly elected president. A very energetic leader he proved to be too, for within three weeks he had personally enrolled 50 life governors, including every Scottish peer in the House of Lords, and had gathered over £500 in subscriptions. Among those first life members were the Duke of Richmond and Gordon, the Duke of Montrose, Lord Lovat, Lord Rosebery, Lord Galloway, Lord Wharncliffe, Lord Strathmore, and the Earl of Dalkeith, with the Prince of Wales being appointed Patron. Altogether the Earl wrote 200 letters requesting support – all in his own hand.

There was good sense and wisdom put forward at that inaugural meeting by John Martin, who called for 'great liberality' on the part of those forming the Stud Book. This was in the matter of receiving pedigrees of somewhat doubtful authenticity. There was propaganda too, with the declaration from him that for the combined qualities of activity, strength and endurance, besides other attributes, there was no breed of horse in the country equal to the Clydesdale, but that if they were to be kept for crossing then they must be kept pure. Significantly neither Drew or Riddell were on that first council, although the first did attend a subsequent meeting. It had been reported that neither of them had made any response; nor did they take notice of either circulars or the move to start a Stud Book.

By the date of the first general meeting, in August 1877, there were £1,000 in life governors' fees, 43 life members and 48 annual subscribers at ten shillings apiece. Registration fees had been fixed at five shillings for stallions and half a crown for mares. John Hendrie was the first secretary but at this date Thomas Dykes took over the post as the first official appointed. The Earl of Dunmore meanwhile had set himself the task of collecting entries for the Stud Book, and with great enthusiasm he soon had 800 clarified and was promising to bring out a retrospective volume for horses foaled by 1st January, 1875, entirely at his own expense. He had two clerks working on it, saying that they were 'up to the necks' in pedigrees. In preparation for the second volume an editing committee was set up, consisting of the Earl and Mr Martin, with W. S. Young of Keir, G. Brown of Shiel, and R. McKean of Lumloch.

There was no mood of euphoria at this stage, surprisingly enough, and indeed within the year cynicism seems to have become widespread with many insisting that the whole organization was running down. This was probably fostered by the fact that there were delays in publication of the Stud Book, and possibly to overcome this Dykes issued a stopgap record of pedigrees. At the same time he pointed out that those who most benefited from pedigree horses were tenant farmers; the very people who had as yet contributed little to the cause.

The problems which the editing committee had to contend with seem to have been daunting; not least because so many horses were given similar names. Many breeders seemed deliberately evasive and did not answer letters, whilst numerous horses had baffling but acceptable aliases, especially stallions which had travelled in different areas of the country and become familiarly known by various descriptions.

It was in December 1878 that the long-awaited Retrospective Stud Book was issued, copies of which are still referred to and valued. Details of 1,044 stallions and 356 mares were listed, and Riddell of course had the largest entry of 64 horses, with friend Drew recording only 11. It was noted that 'relations of the cousinship degree' were common throughout this volume.

From all accounts in fact, a very careful and conscientious job had been done in editing entries, with much recourse to primary sources for checking, and with cards and bills of travelling stallions a help.

This is the first entry in the book, a typical specimen:

A1 1
Brown, Foaled 1869
Bred by John Watson, Edindiach, Gartly, Aberdeenshire.
Property of Alexander Sim, Fawells, Keith Hall, Inverurie,
    Aberdeenshire.
Sire, Eclipse (268), Vol. 1
Dam, pedigree unknown.

At the breed society's annual general meeting in 1879 consideration was given to what was called 'the infinity' of horses named Glancer, Prince of Wales, Champion, and so on, both young and old. It was agreed that these and kindred names should in future be discarded. Scriptural names were also frowned upon, although one member pointed out that Etam, the rock associated with the history of Samson, might be all right.

The following Stud Book came out promptly, with the names of 338 stallions and 461 mares recorded. The Earl of Strathmore was appointed president and Dunmore, such a driving force initially, became much less involved. Dunmore was a lively personality, invariably kilted, and had the remarkable distinction of founding the Shorthorn and Highland Cattle Societies as well as the Clydesdale Horse Society. He must have been highly knowledgeable about early pedigree stock too, for when his herd of top Shorthorns was dispersed in 1875 they averaged £672 – a fortune by today's reckoning. Apparently he went off to America to indulge in big game hunting and work as a Christian Scientist until his death in 1907. There was another change at the end of the same year of 1881 when Dykes went off to London and journalism and Archibald McNeilage was appointed secretary. Now here was a man who was to exert considerable influence in his 50 years in the post. Like Dunmore he was deeply religious, being a Free Church lay preacher, and travelled widely with Stud Book and Bible.

These early years thus saw frequent changes in leadership and a constant struggle to maintain and extend the work of breeding pedigree horses. Underlying all activity was a great uncertainty as to what policy to adopt in the face of continuing pressure for admitting 'foreign' strains such as Drew had infused. For example, in 1883 at the annual general meeting of the English Carthorse Society, a former member of the Clydesdale Horse Society council, Mr Chandos Pole-Gell, put forward the suggestion that there might be one book for Great Britain, on the grounds that England had been drained of its best mares to Scotland. One English horse, Lincolnshire Lad, had bred more winning Clydes than any other in the Kingdom and yet such animals did not rank in the Stud Book sense. John Martin was ready with the defence that the aim was to establish a breed of Clydesdale that would reproduce a particular characteristic of pure-bred certainty. When they had begun the work they had been in the position of having to be satisfied with pedigrees springing from names such as 'Hartley's Blind Horse' and similar; now they were moving to truer pedigrees. According to him the most successful sire of the day had one-sixteenth part of English blood in his veins. Another speaker maintained that there were large numbers of what were called Shire or English cart horses that had the appearance of the Clydesdale, although wanting their impressiveness. It was known that they had been bred with Clyde blood at the bottom or foundation. There was even a horse called 'Tom of the Gills', entered in the English Society's book as a Clydesdale although it was said it had none of the blood in its veins. The matter was eventually settled when the English body voted by 17 to 8 to change its name to that of the Shire Horse Society.

Two months later there was another discomfiting development in that a 'Select Clydesdale Horse Society of Scotland' was formed. It had the declared aim of publishing an 'authentic' stud book, to induce greater competition for breed improvement – rather a cheeky proposal altogether. Behind it was Lawrence Drew, who was chairman, with Davie Riddell a director and James Dunbar as secretary. Ironically enough the first volume, published a year later, contained a preface which was mainly devoted to an obituary for Drew.

This was equally short-lived as a venture, although it seems three stud books were produced up to 1888. 'A very peculiar production' was one comment, probably by McNeilage in his journalistic capacity. He quoted a typical entry as reading: 'A good mare of the right stamp, likely to breed a good colt some day.' Yet for all its critics the 'Select' which was subsequently led by Riddell, drew 340 members and in 1885 registered 250 stallions and 400 mares. Thus its strength was almost equal to that of the Clydesdale Horse Society and proposals for a merger were given consideration. Dunbar as secretary certainly could not be underestimated, because he was a barrister and had conducted numerous cases for Riddell and was later called to the English Bar. His influence can be detected in at least one case abroad, relating to extra-dition proceedings in the States, on petition from Riddell and Raeside of Craigton. The former, incidentally, should not have been flattered by Lord Trayner's remark at the hearing that 'generally speaking horse dealers have not very much character to spare . . .' There were echoes of this in 1891 when a group of Americans were reported to be making an onslaught against the 'Selective Clydesdale Horse Society [sic]' and Riddell, going as far as to declare the book a fraud. However within a year it was reinstated in their eyes and, more important, recognized by the US Government.

Officially nothing came of a suggestion that it would be better called the 'Draught Horse Society' because the intention was to register any horse in the book, irrespective of breed, capable of taking prizes. That would had had the merit of being a completely novel means of regis-tration. Dykes, from London, tried in vain to open up a draught horse register for all stock considered ineligible for Clydesdale, Shire or Suffolk stud books.

The 1880s were a period of considerable growth in exports, whether as a result of breed society efforts or in spite of them. Lord Arthur Cecil, as president, told the annual meeting of 1882 that the fourth volume of the Stud Book contained a large number of entries in American names and thought this was of vast importance, since as with Shorthorn cattle there might be moves to reintroduce some of the fashionable names and breeding back into this country. His prophesy was well-founded, although export fever subsided by the end of the decade.

It is likely that the export boom which developed was, in part, responsible for as many worthless pedigrees being issued, to boost the values of the horses. So the task of editing the Stud Book in those early days was not an enviable one, and would have gained small thanks from fellow breeders, for numerous horses were turned down for registration and at one stage it was freely admitted that because of shipments abroad, some of the best animals left in the home country were unregistered and ineligible. This was also true of those taking the honours at the shows. At the 21st Stallion Show, for example, with all the best horses away overseas and even Riddell's customary large entry absent, the three highest premiums went to sires which were all ineligible. The previous year Joseph Bulloch's horse Zulu, by Lord Lyon, had won the major premium and yet been rejected for registration because of obscurities in the dam's pedigree.

An indication of the nature of the problems encountered can be gauged from the enquiry by a member as to what to do when he found his horse had travelled widely for four years, and the groom had given him a name different from that registered. The number of entries to be corrected worldwide, changing the name on the pedigrees of the stock Hattonslap Chief sired to Lord Falconer, must have tried tempers sorely.

There was, however, increasing confidence within the breed at this period, which is reflected also in John Martin's speech to a meeting in 1889. He declared: 'From whatever source the Clydesdales came originally they are now a breed equal to any in the world. Whether what was known as the Shire horses were originally the same as Scotch horses – whether originally they derived their best breeding stock from Scotland, or we from them, need not be considered.' He continued: 'Those who say they are the same breed now would do well to visit a show of Clydesdales, then go to Islington to see the Shires, then if they know anything about horses they will be able to see for themselves whether they are the same breed or not.'

The start of the next decade brought many changes to the Clydesdale Society. In 1890 with the collapse of American demand for stallions, the whole business had become depressed with a loss of £456 on the year's accounts. When things begin to go badly critics never fail to appear and they were never wanting among the Clydesdale men. In fact things were going so badly in the USA that the breed secretary's salary was cut by half, and there was sniping that the cost of keeping a highly-paid secretary to boss a single clerk could not be afforded. Actually the salary was fixed at £150 per annum two years later, when it was discovered that McNeilage had voluntarily foregone £50 for the previous ten years. Presumably in order to reduce overheads he was also allowed to act as secretary to Hackney horse breeders. More serious was the charge, made in familiar terms, that the society was running a closed shop as regards selection for exports, and changes in the rules were demanded. This was when annual members were permitted to join Council, and the membership became organized into districts to ensure fairer representation.

Once again the demand for a crossbred horse register re-opened, with oddly enough McNeilage himself advocating this in 1895 to ensure the blending of Shire and Clydesdale blood for draught purposes. Colourfully he predicted the outcome as 'producing geldings which would lick Creation!' Adding to confusion was the voice of a newcomer to Council urging that stock by registered Clydesdale stallions out of registered Shire mares or vice versa should be allowed to register in the Stud Book and given a distinctive mark. These demands were persistently made and it says much for the stalwarts in office that they resisted all suggestions, and even in 1906 decided to be more stringent about the rules. Instead of insisting on a minimum of three registered crosses it was raised to four. It was pointed out that 'irregular' pedigrees stated to have derived from horses bred on Merryton lines were by then rapidly dying out.

A new show competition was established in 1891 with the gift by the Earl of Cawdor of 100gns for the purchase of two trophies to be awarded in his name, for the best in each sex annually. These were to become famed as the blue riband of the Clydesdale breed and have remained in perpetual competition, although of course the original cups have long since been replaced.

Royal interest in Clydesdales was maintained, with Queen Victoria becoming a patron in 1892. King Edward VII bought a mare for Balmoral stud soon after he succeeded and there was great satisfaction that a Baron's Pride foal could be expected.

It was in 1895, with Vol. 17 at half the normal size, that the breed really had to face up to cutbacks. Elaborate offices in a fashionable city street were vacated in favour of less space up a stair in an office block. The mighty had fallen in many eyes. There was also a rumpus when the question was raised of later generation Clydesdales returning from America and not strictly speaking being eligible for the Stud Book back home. This arose through William Montgomery's proposed purchase of Colonel Holloway's stallion Prince of Quality, and with feelings so high registration was denied. The horse had to be resold in preference to facing a boycott of the stock.

The biggest row of all time was at the AGM in 1897 when it was mooted that the rules should be changed to allow horses other than pure-bred Clydesdales to register. An appendix for part-breds was proposed. It was felt that the timing for such a radical move might be right at last, for it could help to ease the financial burden. Feelings in fact ran so high that there were several members with legal advisors present at the meeting, and at various points in the debate there were reported 'loud cries of No, No.' and groans and even hisses were heard. The meeting resulted in tightening up rules for registration rather than easing them.

Competition as well as feelings were running high at this point. English horse breeders got a taste of it when in 1899 HRH the Prince of Wales attended the Highland Show and the Shire men sent up entries for the first time ever, including the Royal personage's own first-prize colt from the breed show, and the champion gelding. The classes then of course were of mixed stock but Clydesdale men were judging, as might have been expected, and perhaps it was not surprising that the Sandringham horses were not even commended, and the champion Shire only managed third prize. So angry were Shire exhibitors that they threatened to see the Royal Show of England did not cater any more for Clydesdales.

There was heated debate on another topic about this period, veterinary inspection of prize stock. Not only was doctoring creeping in – not for the first time – but there was serious concern also about infertility in top stallions. One great winner was described as having been 'cast [put down] by a munificent friend and patron of the vet. concerned' and there were numerous incidents of the kind. It was in 1908 that veterinary inspection was made a condition of winning major trophies and this was hailed as a big step forward. By this time, incidentally, the fourth set of Cawdor Cups was being bought, and so it was decided to ensure that outright success became more difficult (they were expensive) and evidence of fertility was made a condition too.

This was the time at which A. and W. Montgomery made application for the exclusive use of the prefix or affix 'Baron' for their stud. It was to make history. At this time the only names recorded were 'Gartly' by A. Mennie; 'Montrave' by Sir John Gilmour, and 'Silver' by Seaham Harbour studs, together with the first and last 'Scottish' from Sinclair Scott.

Whether due to gathering war clouds or not, there started another period of phenomenal prosperity in heavy horses and in 1910 the Clydesdales had a best-ever year. Exports totalled 1,531 head, membership stood at 1,854 and there was £7,235 capital at credit. As the annual report proudly declared: 'The breed of Clydesdale horse is now become a worldwide industry.' In fact the majority of exports were to Canada, with breeders there demanding that every animal be numbered in the Stud Book, including both parents. As a small acknowledgement of the way in which Canadians had patronized their horses, the Society's council invested £1,000 in Canadian securities.

By 1912 the Stud Book total had reached 6,461 entries – another record. There were problems a year later when a Cart Horse Stud Book, operated by H. R. Burgess from Teignmouth, Devonshire, came into being, although few reckoned the introduction was serious. Council was actually more pre-occupied with finance, turning down a move to vote themselves expense allowances by 40 votes to eight. Shire breeders meanwhile were resolved to spend £2,000 on publicity over the next five years, rather than give council members fees.

During World War I the Clydesdale, along with other heavy horse breeds, made an enormous contribution and one not sufficiently recognized now that we are living in a mechanized age. A later chapter describes this role more fully but here it is enough to point to enormous demand and every effort being made to meet it. When J. E. Kerr of Harviestoun took the presidency over in 1916, membership had reached 2,662 and was to peak at 3,930 members in 1922.

An event of unusual significance at this stage was a meeting with the committee of the Shire Horse Society; not, it must be said hastily, to arrange a merger, but at least to consider ways of working together. It showed a remarkable change in attitude and both were agreed on the need to put unsound stallions off the road, probably because this had become a matter of urgency after wartime breeding regardless of quality factors. Echoes of this are seen also in reports from Canada and in 1920 Andrew Graham said in Manitoba that the home society had to help owners there, and he cited the fact that all the leading winners at Toronto had been 'blanks' at home. One impassioned plea was made in these words: 'You must destroy or castrate your rubbishy horses at home; we don't want them out here!'

For those noting the statistics the 42nd volume of the Clydesdale Stud Book was the biggest ever with 6,879 entries, compared with 5,280 in 1916. Agricultural returns for England and Wales recorded a 25,000 reduction in horses kept for farm work. The Percheron had by now become the most popular breed in the USA, with the majority of farmers there preferring them, although Canada was up to 75 per cent loyal to the Clydesdale. The cry was the familiar one of 'Keep the lorry in view' and the complaint that weight and substance were being sacrificed to pretty looks.

The breed society's silver jubilee in 1927 was a grand affair, even if exports were by then down to 130 horses and membership falling fast. The Duke of Montrose presided over a celebratory dinner and there was keen disappointment that the sole surviving founder councillor, John Clay, could not be there. He had become one of the Chicago stockyard kings, and it was only discovered too late that he was in Europe at the time. Writing from Florence, Clay said that helping to found the society had been his proudest moment, adding praise for Glasgow Corporation whose refuse collectors had one time turned out 337 cart geldings in great order, and he still remembered it with pride. Nostalgic reminiscence has always been a feature of heavy horse functions, when bibulous strong men weep, so to speak, and this one was no exception. One of the signatories to the original Memorandum of Association, it transpired, was Colonel Robert Lloyd-Lindsay (later Lord Wantage), owner of one of the most influential Shire horse studs in the country.

Possibly it was the echoes of this celebration which helped to stimulate interest; at any rate a wider appreciation of the Clydesdale resulted from that point on, and for the first time ever the breed as such was recognized at the Highland Show of 1928, separate classes being granted. There were, to be sure, rumblings of discontent that Shires were given similar honour – mitigated doubtless by Captain A. H. Clark, a Shire man, enthusing over the Clydesdale's beautiful lines and hair and even going so far as to suggest that it might be a helpful influence on his own breed. It evened things up when he added that, conversely, a dash of Shire influence might give the Clyde more courage and constitution, and help get rid of its extreme artificiality of foot. That last crack was not well received; nor was Edmund Beck's quip that whilst Scotsmen had guts their Clydesdales had none.

Many of the pioneers of the modern horse passed away in the next few years, including John Findlay who bred Baron's Pride at Springhill, a man who was a noted critic of breed society finances and conducted a protracted argument with the Inland Revenue which brought the societies lasting tax relief. William Elliot, founder of the great Lanark sales was another, and his reputation was said to have been respected by all honest men and held in wholesome dread by rogues. James Weir of Sandilands Stud was described at a presentation dinner by the Earl of Home as being 'one of the great makers' of the Clydesdale. Many would love the epitaph. Weir's recollections of shows went back to 1857, remarkably, and he used to recall the leading stallion Merry Tom (532), a big plain grey horse owned by Charles Philips of Cracrop, who walked him all the way from Carlisle. That in itself seems a notable marathon record.

McNeilage had a half century in office before he died in 1932, being succeeded by Samuel Mackenzie who had 58 years in the breed's service but was secretary for only six years. Then Robert Jarvis, an estate factor, was appointed out of 45 applicants. There was another example of long service when Matthew Mitchell retired as auditor in 1946 after 54 years' tenure. The men were as hardy as their horses.

Few give the heavy horses any mention so far as World War II was concerned, although they did work extensively on the land and in haulage. Even by 1939 official statistics were telling a story of steady decline in agricultural use, with the total for Great Britain down to the lowest recorded 100,900 and still dropping away. Unlike World War I there was no immediate post-war slump of massive account but there were dramatic switches to motors. The railway companies for example dispersed their stocks, and the L.N.E.R. in Glasgow alone had a final parade of 198 head. Vast numbers went for slaughter and some indication is given in Canadian reports of orders for 40,000 horses going into Europe, mainly, thank goodness, for work in France, but 10,000 tons of horse-meat for human needs went into Belgium.

In the face of such trends it is interesting that society membership rose, even whilst Volume 54 of the Stud Book in 1947 showed the lowest-ever entry of 1,438. It was not until 1950 that support melted away, and then to an extent which occasioned much concern; stud books became amalgamated with talk of preserving specimens of stock in the museums and other collections. But still if the annual accounts were into the red, there were ample reserves and the diehards were determined to run the organization at a loss for as long as funds remained.

In the event this was not necessary, for the nadir was reached quickly and a new subsidy scheme to aid native horse breeds and their support was founded by the Horserace Betting Levy Board or 'the Tote' in recognition of their contribution to racing. It was a massive help to survival and even by 1953 there were the first signs that the decline had been arrested; actually they came when at an international ploughing match it was noted that for every spectator standing around the latest model tractors there would be a dozen watching the few remaining plodding horses. The tide was turning and indeed the enthusiasm which never quite sparked out soon rekindled itself and scarcity created demand.

With the centenary annual general meeting of the Clydesdale Horse Society in 1976 came the long-awaited report that membership was slowly rising again, and investments still stood at £13,000. Better still was the news that the export demand for horses of the right type was greater than could be supplied. It was a real moment of triumph, and one to savour as the first inklings of a coming energy crisis promised a vindication for all who had claimed that the heavy horse would be needed once again. The guardians of the breed standards and stud book system had every reason to feel proud of what had been achieved.

Four

Foundation Stock

Powerhouses. Symbols of energy and strength. That is how many see the heavy horses, and in earlier days these were attributes of necessity to cope with the work on the farms, or haulage in the cities. Realizing this, we can better appreciate the excitement that was engendered by the new type as represented by the Clydesdale horse, with its fleetness of foot and active gait. For many these qualities might compare with driving a car after having worked with trucks. Breeders on their part were influenced by the fact that improved type and performance were reflected in high prices and fashionable demand, and nothing is better calculated to spur to greater effort. It is not an exaggeration to state that both came the way of those skilled in producing the right types of horses.

Not that you would expect general agreement on the subject of course. Lord Dunmore's enthusiasm for the first Stud Book was prompted by his concern that breeders such as Lawrence Drew were recklessly infusing English blood into Clydesdale stock, without regard for the consequences. A reasonably accurate view of how the two breeds in Britain complemented one another is given in this report of 1881: 'The blood of the Shire gives increased girth, spring of rib, increase in size, better knee action and freedom from founder; on the other hand the Clydesdale gives clean bones, quickness in work, a beautiful head and eye, and a sound enduring constitution.'

The older judges in earlier days apparently felt that the stock differed little from those they recalled seeing at fairs in their youth. But in fact they were reluctant to concede, as the knowledgeable often are, that there had been 40 years of steady improvement. Size was increased, although in some instances resulting in legginess. Typical, too, was a comment made after the national show of 1871 when one breeder thought the Clydesdales 'somewhat deficient in stoutness' for breeding weight-carrying hunters.

While master breeders such as Drew undoubtedly crossed with forethought and skill, there were others less discriminating. Fears were expressed that all manner of horses were being bred from Clydesdale and Suffolk breeds, and being crossed and recrossed down to none-descripts until it was impossible to know what breed predominated. Clydes crossed with 'old N.B. mares' were frequently praised, perhaps because they had a line or two of Cleveland coach horses in their make-up.

What was a good type of Clydesdale? This description dating back to 1873 gives a useful guide:

Standing at least 16.5 hands high, with a pretty large head, pleasant face, thick neck, wide breast and heavy upright shoulders. A broad, short back, strong loins, deep chest, round and full flanks, broad and well-rounded quarters, muscular thighs and forearms, large and clean hocks and knee joints, short leg bones with full tendons behind, short strong pasterns, deep sound feet. The forelegs should be well apart and well under the body, from which they should descend in a perpendicular direction when the horse is at ease.

Breeders always did have a tendency to carry some show features to extremes, especially when it came to head or hocks. A narrow head with no room for brains has often been condemned, with a medium-size and broad forehead with large open nostrils preferred. A bold and honest eye well set could indicate the docile and wise horse that might be easily trained; whereas the narrow forehead with small deep-set eye could betoken one of nervous disposition.

It matters how the head is set on to the neck, because balance and pulling power can depend on it. The long and arched, well set-on shoulder, deep and slanting and more oblique than in the Shire, has been a distinctive Clydesdale feature that contributed much to the long, quick step which has caught the attention. The English cart horse's more upright shoulder tended to give greater 'collar power' but was too often accompanied by the short, slow step. And very essential to sound action was the strong, straight forearm loaded with strong muscle for full power, and with that feature, the broad chest resulting from a large and well constructed body.

A point not readily appreciated is that much depends on a horse possessing a sound back. Over the years this feature has been endlessly debated, with some declaring that undue length was a fault; others liked particularly the stallion to have a short-coupled back. Slackness of the back, between the withers and croup, was generally regarded by English and Americans alike as being a distinctive Clydesdale fault but the Scots' view was that the back never broke and a short, strong

45

one with long quarters was best.

The real fetish however, lay with the Clydesdales' legs. To this day it never fails to fascinate visitors to see the scene in any show-ring when exhibitors will be gathered around the legs and feet of their charges, combing out the hair and generally fussing over every detail. The sound leg has plenty of good flat bone beneath the knee, because experience has shown that those with soft, round legs and ill-defined sinews simply do not stand up to hard work. Short upright pasterns are criticized for impeding action. In the hind-quarters, breadth and low setting must be accompanied by muscular thighs descending down into broad well-developed hocks.

There has always been fury engendered over whether or not hocks with moderate bend gave better propelling power. The veterinarian T. Campbell, back in 1894, declared that the straight hock with a prominence of the astragalus bones was often found on what were dubbed the' best Clydesdales, although actually they had a malformation from hock to foot which produced a weakness of pastern. The best, he contended, had a perfectly angled hock with no swelling or spavin in front, and a beautiful oblique angle from top of fetlock to hoof.

In similar vein the outstanding veterinarian Professor J. R. M'Call once critized the other extreme: 'We have a number of massive good stallions of the breed, whose faces are unknown in the show-ring simply because they do not close their hocks sufficiently to please the fastidious autocrats.' A sound view, as it happens, because this fad continued well into the '20s with very close action behind and hocks almost rubbing together and quite unsound.

Overseas buyers of horses have always exerted a sound influence on type standards, even if breeders pretended not to heed them. In the peak exporting year of 1912, for example, Australian and New Zealand buyers were inclined to laugh at efforts to produce 'tall' horses and from all quarters of the globe came complaints against show-type extremes. The summary of what was sought in a good draught horse capable of work was soundness in feet and limbs, deep well-ribbed barrel, powerfully developed forearms and thighs, long quarters and short back, intelligent head and good, straight action; more pleasing in perfection when walking then in giving a showy display at the trot.

Then there was the question of hair. Now it may not be thought that this was of any significance – the long hair or feather on the legs, called the 'spat' or 'gaiter', endlessly combed out and resined to perfection. It was the groom's pride that it be long, straight and silky. The Americans, in particular, were otherwise minded and condemned what they called 'the rage for rank feather' as a bother to ploughmen. Little notice was taken – the fashion lives on today.

46

Colour has always been another question. Deep brown was the preference, especially if dappled, but breeders were wary of chestnut as of doubtful origin and roan was also considered impure, but a stripe of 'ratch' or white on the face was highly sought. Grey was one of the old Clydesdale colours, but very early on Frame of Broomfield showed complete antipathy to it, sacrificing every foal of that description no matter how good. Others followed the example, with the result that whereas greys had been common enough they were soon virtually eliminated. Charles Philips' Merry Tom (532), described as the best looking and worst breeding stallion ever to gain the Glasgow Show prize, won the Highland 1854 and Royal 1855 and he was a grey – as were many top Cumberland stallions of the day. There was a race of grey Glenelgs from Durham which won freely and travelled widely. Robert Wilson had a grey Comet (192), said to have had a lasting influence, but only one pure white (technically grey) foal has been noted, and that was born on Arran in 1923.

Type and colour tend to be fads and varying influences on a breed which change through time; whereas basic soundness is the all-constant factor. If extremes were to be found in prize studs it was draught or working standards which counted most. In this respect a government Horse Breeding Act of 1920 exerted profound influence for good, in that no entire horse was allowed to travel on stud duties without a licence given after inspection. The aim was to drive the unsound sires off the road, and it manifestly had an impact with 80 refused licence in the first year, due to defects, and within five years the failure rate was down to 17 refusals. Roaring or whistling, i.e. wind faults, were commonest and breed type or fertility were of no account – noticeably at least. Heavy horse breeding grants were also an inducement towards improvement, if for no other reason than that they were instrumental in giving small farmers access to good stallions for their few mares on reasonable terms. When they were withdrawn in Scotland in 1931 the effect was serious; conversely continuity in England and Wales up to 1939 was extremely valuable. Actually they were revived in 1942 at £40 a stallion, and only ceased finally in 1957 by which time, in the North at least, only 16 stallions were engaged and these travelled by lorry. The stirring sight of the stallion man and his charge on the road had gone.

The impression may be that Clydesdale breeders followed fashion slavishly and often lost their way in show points, incidental to overall improvement. This was true but should not disguise the fact that the master breeders began with an ill-assorted type and mixed strains, which hardly constituted a breed. They got short-term rapid improvement in the hybrid vigour resultant from infusing Shire blood, but the

47

real skill was in fixing this improvement into later generations –
effectively establishing the breed.

Geneticists have over the years shown keenest interest in the way in
which this miracle was wrought, usually agreeing that it was done
within a time span of some 60 years, and as a result of line breeding
closely to the Darnley strain. This was made possible as there was
heavy use of such top stallions, most of which had similar recurrent
strains within their pedigree blood lines. In-breeding was a constant
risk, but although studs sailed close to the wind on occasions the
skilful manipulation of the genes maintained steady improvement.
How this was done, and the stock which contributed so much to it,
comes through in successive chapters.

Five

The Super Studs

Relatively few Clydesdale horses proved to have a very profound influence on the breed, so it is no wonder that they were revered or that their names live on in the memory of enthusiasts. Such stallions had a charisma comparable only to that of contemporary pop music or sporting heroes and manifestly did much to lighten the dreary drag of labour on the land, not least in the improvement progeny gave to the means of tilling it.

Prince of Wales was the first of the great horses that caught public interest, being used widely and thus represented strongly by prize stock. One stalwart, Quintin Dunlop, counted it an honour that he had actually been present at the birth of such an animal. Once mature they used to say Prince of Wales stepped out like a trotting horse, so that standing behind one could see the soles of his feet every time they were lifted. Still it was a myth that he was unbeaten at any show – he lost the crown on at least two occasions. The description 'almost perfect' was most apt.

There is no doubt, however, that Prince of Wales' procreative powers were well tried, if not exploited, and the stud fee of £40 in 1876 was big money – not at all comparable with the 22s 6d charged for his grandsire, Sir Walter Scott. But his two-year-olds were selling for £3,000 and yearlings £2,000 apiece, paid it is believed for Prince of Albion (6178) who set a breed record of four successive wins at the national show; and Prince of Kyle (7155) – both bred by R. F. F. Campbell MP, of Craigie. Another of his sons was Cedric (1087), bred by Professor M'Call who sold to Colonel Holloway in America. Even at 17 years this horse's movement was described as unforgettable. This was the term used for another son, Prince of Avondale, but it appeared that his groom at Merryton had perfected it by schooling over a track built of railway sleepers.

A daughter of Prince of Wales, called Young Rosie, was actually considered to be even better than her sire, which was praise indeed. She won top show honours and bred one outstanding foal in Prince Charlie by Old Times. He in turn got the most famous mare of all in Moss Rose (6203), bred by the ironfounder George Ure of Wheatlands and his only venture ever into the breeding of Clydesdales. When Sir John Gilmour paid 1,000gns for her in 1885 for his Montrave Stud it was described as 'the longest price ever' for a female of the breed; worth it, though, because it was generally agreed that there was not a single weakness in the mare and she was to dominate the best lines in the future. There was a historic judging occasion in 1893 at the Highland Show when Moss Rose's daughter Queen of the Roses won the Cawdor Cup for females, with another daughter, Montrave Maud, in reserve place. Then the old mare at 13 years came out and beat both of them.

With confusing hyperbole Darnley (222) was also dubbed 'sire of the century'. He was foaled in 1872 at Sir William Stirling Maxwell's Keir Stud. The sire was Conqueror (199) by happy accident, because the dam, Keir Peggy, would not settle to the chosen stud and it was as last resort that she was stood to what was described as 'an old thief of a horse' travelling the district. Be that as may, meticulous research proved Darnley to be carefully line-bred back to the oldest of Clydesdale stock, with pedigree traceable back on seven distinct strains to the sire of Broomfield Champion, and of course his dam was even more closely bred and gave remarkable uniformity.

That Darnley had influence is evident from the fact that of 46 stallions on the road in 1888 he had 14 sons, 13 grandsons and 4 great-grandsons. His stock was closely linked to A. and W. Montgomery's famed Netherhall Stud. Major influence on the modern Clydesdale can be traced in the Baron's Pride (9122) line of Sir Everard (5353). He was twice beaten at shows and carpers said he had a pony's head.

There was a notable grandson of Darnley in Montrave Mac (9958) by McGregor, costing £1,000 as a two-year-old and still working at 27 years. This horse bred many good mares, one of which, Poor Girl, lived 30 years and had 14 foals with seven in succession to Baron's Pride; in fact she founded an entire stud and held the record for longevity. In breeding terms J. E. Kerr's Ambrosine did better with eight successive foals to Baron's Pride and then five to Footprint.

The new luminary, Baron's Pride, foaled in 1890 in R. and J. Findlay's Springhill Stud, had a most unfortunate debut, being unplaced in show and described as 'effeminate'; but one year later the shrewd William Montgomery saw his potential for he was bought along with another horse for £400, and having shaken hands on the deal the vendor was told to keep the stable-mate.

What the experts of old claimed for Baron's Pride was that the horse demonstrated the great 'wearing qualities' of the Clydesdale breed. But more objectively the stallion's real worth was in breeding phenomenally, and the Montgomery were well placed to exploit him. Still one has a suspicion that fame retrospectively rests with siring the legendary Baron of Buchlyvie (11263), and his story comes later. For a horse lacking weight and substance Baron's Pride remarkably extended the championship lines of both sexes. He died in 1912 and over years it was counted a privilege to get a nomination.

Geneticists have for long looked with interest on a horse called Hiawatha (10067) bred by William Hunter of Garthland off a Prince of Wales' son Prince Robert. Matt. Marshall bought him as a foal and sold to John Pollock of Papermill Stud, where he proved all but sterile in early years. But he won the Cawdor Cup four times, when that was possible, and set a new standard in perfect legs. Better still he bred what was termed 'the truest and best-moulded mare' of the breed in 40 years. This was Boquhan Lady Peggie, who, alas, died with her first foal. Breeding interest lay in the Hiawatha cross on Baron's Pride and Sir Everard mares; interestingly Marshall bought mares from Sir Robert Gunterson, Wetherby, and the Duke of Leeds, to test this cross the reverse way.

One horse which was back to Hiawatha was J. and P. Donald's Fyvie Sensation (20042), that went to Netherhall and bred the great breeding and show stallion Benefactor (20867), sold for 4,400gns at the Sandy-knowe dispersal. He died in 1952.

When it comes to super-stallions there will never be one to beat Baron of Buchlyvie, closely followed by his son Dunure Footprint. The dramas surrounding them illustrate the rivalry and dogmatism of master breeders, with fortunes and fame at stake, not to mention the constant goal of show success and the pursuit of perfection.

Baron of Buchlyvie, son of Baron's Pride, was spotted as a yearling by James Kilpatrick of Craigie Mains, and a subsequent £700 deal plus a gelding for luck was considered ample for a rather under-sized colt, narrow and lacking strength of bone. It was made a joint purchase with William Dunlop of Dunure and it appeared that what had attracted their admiration was the extremely fine quality of bone and hair – the latter hung like silk. As the horse grew he improved wondrously, finishing a handsome 2,000lb and winning well.

The horse was stood at Dunure, apparently after Dunlop had bought out Kilpatrick for £2,000 but whether or not this was ever agreed became a cause célèbre which echoed round the world. First Lord Skerrington in the High Court decided in favour of Kilpatrick, then it was reversed in favour of Dunlop as sole owner and then Kilpatrick took it to the House of Lords which eventually agreed the original decision, leaving the horse as joint property of the two litigants.

Remarkable evidence came to light, including the fact that Dunlop kept no current account in any bank; instead he carried his pounds in his pockets. Giving judgement the Lord Chancellor, the Earl of Halsbury, was outspoken: 'I am seldom called upon to decide in a case in which I feel so strongly that on one side or the other there has been abominable wickedness.' The Solicitor General had appeared for Dunlop and on the outcome Kilpatrick had been awarded his expenses, reckoned to be not far short of three times the original price paid for the horse i.e. over £2,000.

So the partnership had to be dissolved and an auction sale at Ayr market on 14th December 1911 was decided upon. On that day the crowd was so vast that many could not get within sight of the sale-ring and it was doubted whether there had ever been such a gathering in the whole history of horse breeding. The now 12-year-old horse was led in, looking impressive but apparently needing all his weight, and it was only a matter of minutes until a stranger acting for Dunlop bid the price up to £9,500. Cordial cheering met the world record and acknowledged the end of a protracted quarrel, although it has to be said that the combatants did not exchange a word in the next 22 years.

Bearing in mind that the current equivalent of such a price would certainly be £250,000 it is hardly surprising that even the Americans thought the deal fictitious, believing that earning capacity determined an animal's value. The stallion's earnings approximated from £2,000 to as high as £3,000 after the case; but two and a half years later, following a kick from a mare, Baron of Buchlyvie had to be put down. The skeleton is on permanent display in Glasgow's principal museum.

Dunlop was honoured in 1912 by fellow breeders in appreciation of his efforts to improve agricultural horses, and in a speech he acknowledged that he had overstepped the bounds of sanity but he could not have rested without possessing the Baron. There was a sequel in fact, for although Dunlop had claim on any foal by the Baron one was sold to Kilpatrick privily, which resulted in a claim being put into Court. It was apparently settled by arbitration and the horse, named Craigie Litigant (19071) proved to be outstanding for Kilpatrick's stud, winning the Cawdor Cup in 1918, and £10,000 was offered for him as a three-year-old. Oddly enough he died young and so both litigants suffered similar loss.

If ever a stallion was exploited it was certainly Dunure Footprint (15203) son of the Baron of Buchlyvie, and Dunlop named him after that line in Longfellow's *Psalm of Life* – 'Footprints on the sands of time' so convinced was he that this was his ideal horse. Although un-

remarkable in his show career the stallion swiftly established a reputation as stud horse as breeders sought the Darnley–B.Pride–Baron
blood lines he represented. The result was that at the height of his
season Footprint was serving a mare every two hours day and night,
and it took the milk of two cows, countless eggs and heaven knows what
else to sustain the effort. Terms were 6ogns at service and 6ogns when
a mare was proved in foal, so the financial reckoning was enormous.

In later years as stories circulated, people began to doubt the truth
of this horse's libido, but plenty of evidence came forward to support
it. There were those who recalled seeing as many as 18 mares at a time
come off the train in a day and go up to the Dunure farm. A one-time
groom recalled arriving with a mare and being awakened at 2 am to be
told that it was the mare's turn – that was at the start of the season in
April and even so the mare was the hundredth to visit Footprint. When
Dunlop's accounts were seen later, for the year 1921, it showed stallion
fees amounting to £9,690, and Footprint was mentioned as having made
£15,000 in two seasons. Stud books confirmed it with Vol. 42 registering
121 foals in 1919 and to this must be added foals born dead or lost and
those not registered at all, plus an allowance for repeat services. Vol. 39
listed 146 foals as produce, indicating 200–300 mares a season.

As a footnote it may be wondered why the stallion's mother bred
nothing similar, since he was a first foal. The record showed Dunure
Index, died aged four; Black Silk went to Mr J. P. Sleigh; Dunure
Chosen won the Cawdor Cup; Keynote was a fair winner; then two
barren seasons and finally death after foaling. The mare was ranked
amongst the best of her breed, but chance and luck play their part.

Six

Master Breeders

Although it is the case that one or two outstanding studs, and more especially their top sires, dominated the Clydesdale breed, there has always been significant contribution from a wide range of enthusiasm. Individuals today tend to have no more than one or two mares as a hobby; where once horse-breeding was a massive enterprise. But then of course the horse was the means of transport and husbandry, and therefore of the greatest national importance.

The role of Sir John Gilmour, politician and landowner of high standing, has been mentioned briefly and deservedly too as one who made a great contribution to the Clydesdale. Very much involved with public bodies, he served on a Royal Commission which effected much improvement in breeding better horses. His own stud set a good example and was involved in many huge transactions for the times. In 1885, for instance, he bought the mare Moss Rose from Montgomery for £1,000. Then three years later the stallion Prince of Albion from Kilpatrick for a record £3,000. And he sold stock from Montrave to extend its influence worldwide, including in 1892 a two-year-old filly, Queen of the Roses, for which Montgomery paid 1,000gns. His famous mare Vanda by Hiawatha was probably a great bargain, sold as a seven-year-old to McLean of Medrox for 626gns. The stud was dispersed in 1914, when 14 horses averaged £159 – and that must have been a disappointment.

Veterinary influence in the early days was highly significant, which explains why Principal James M'Call's name is linked with Clydesdale history. He farmed at Carmunnock, going into Gallowhill in 1865. His father had been a carrier and his brother was a Chief Constable of city police forces, whilst his own career was quite remarkable: he began as apprentice lawyer, then went to London and was eventually put in charge of Pickford's stables of 1,000 work horses. Becoming interested in the physiological problems associated with such a number, he began a study of the veterinary side. Colic cases were numerous amongst horses under his care and M'Call set about seeking remedies, and introduced the nosebag as a means of stopping a ravenous horse returning to stables and gorging itself. When he returned to his native country, he enrolled at Edinburgh Veterinary School, and is thought to have held a Chair in Anatomy there, before entering practice in Glasgow and opening classes in veterinary science. This tale well illustrates how veterinary care developed and indeed M'Call was instrumental in applying for Glasgow's Royal Charter in 1862, which was opposed by the only other colleges in London and Edinburgh. Doggedly he won through and his work in testing unsound horses out of shows undoubtedly did much to raise standards. Although twice vice-president of the breed society, he only briefly held the presidency – although he may well have declined it previously. He did breed one good horse, Cedric (1087) which went to America. Twice married, M'Call had 16 children and having five sons qualify as veterinary surgeons must be a record!

One undoubted master and quiet influence touching a wide variety of livestock was J. Ernest Kerr of Harviestoun. A remarkable man, he bred six Cawdor Cup winners: 1908, Nerissa by Baron's Pride – she went to British Columbia; 1912, Scotland Yet (14839) the stallion and Harviestoun Baroness (another B. Pride) the female winner; 1913, Phyllis, full sister to Scotland Yet; 1913, Flashdale – a great sire; 1930, Alanna. Throughout a long life Ernest Kerr stuck rigidly to principles and never had a stallion heading his stud – instead mares were sent out. This was because he believed that no single horse existed which was right for different sorts of mares and which would earn recognition at shows from different judges. All the work on his farms was done by geldings, because he considered breeding stock too valuable to be put at risk. This perhaps explains why one American visitor remarked particularly that on visiting Harviestoun he had seen a mare of 19, two of 18 and another at 14 years old amongst the stock of 12, each of which had foals.

Kerr was a superb stockman, perhaps the greatest in the world, because he had equal success with Shetland ponies, Aberdeen-Angus and Shorthorn cattle, Border Leicester sheep, Ayrshire dairy cows, all kinds of poultry and pheasants, guinea-pigs and Highland terriers. Even in breeding rabbits he would go to great lengths to secure his ideal.

Keir Stud, owned by Sir William Stirling Maxwell, had an early role in breed foundation, but the owner was more active in politics than horses. All the same, when it was dispersed in 1896 some 900 people sat down to the pre-sale luncheon, even if they only paid on average £67 11s 6d a head for the 53 horses. The explanation appears to have been that remarkable prejudice existed against one called Newhope, used in the stud. This is an instance of how support could be denied particular lines, and that despite the fact that on the sale day W. S. Young is supposed to have refused 1,000gns for a Newhope mare and Montrave had taken a stallion at 700gns.

A good example of how patronage could help upgrade horse stocks is found in Sir Michael Shaw Stewart's example at Ardgowan. He invested heavily in stallions and gave liberal premiums for use by his tenants. He was breed society president in 1882 and a great enthusiast and exhibitor.

John Pollock of Papermill is a name woven into history. A kenspeckle figure in an old 'pot' hat with square jaw set firmly, they used to say that his comments on men and matters were seldom restrained and occasionally good to hear. He also had many good horses and was highly knowledgeable about them.

For more than three decades Robert Park of Brunstane Stud will be found in the record books. He bred a two-year-old filly, Rosadora by Marmion (which went to Canada) and won many prizes in 1905. In 1927 his stallion, Brunstane Again (20717) by Footprint, won the Highland Show whilst his daughter, Brunstane Phyllis, won the Cawdor Cup – just beaten for the female title which would have given Park a tremendous double. Phyllis went to J. Torrance, of Markham, Ontario, and promptly won a grand championship at Toronto Winter Fair.

What was even more remarkable about Brunstane, however, was that Park's twin daughters, Mattie and Jean, developed an uncommonly keen eye for stock. Now women were supposedly not 'liberated' at that time and certainly played no active role in the exclusively male province of heavy horse breeding, yet at quite a young age the twins were invited to judge and did so most competently. The stud was dispersed in 1934 when 16 horses averaged £73 8s 8d and 16 years later when Park was honoured by fellow breeders it was reckoned that he had judged Clydesdales more than 600 times. In a speech well seasoned with experience, he reminded a large company that Montgomery had always said that a horse standing more than 17 hands high was all the worse for it.

The small farm of Lumloch, close to Lenzie, was once very important to the Clydesdale, for there Robert McKean had a good eye for a winner. Many came from Campbeltown where Mrs Snodgrass of Clochkeil had a stallion, Largs Jock (444) that was sometimes known as 'Campbell's straight-legged' one. McKean showed Prince Albert (613) to win well and sold him to Lord Wantage to found a stud in Berkshire.

It was said that none did more to popularize the breed abroad, or dealt in as many prize-winners, as did Andrew Montgomery of Netherhall fame. The stock came to prominence through females bred to

Darnley. He bought MacGregor as a yearling in 1879 and this horse had so much influence that at the Chicago World Fair in 1893, practically all the winners were bought from Montgomery and of this line. He was joined as partner by William Montgomery and the enterprise flourished, but still it was always thought that luck led to calling at Springhill Farm, and the purchase of Baron's Pride – reputedly for £400. By all accounts William was a shrewd businessman and their farms were a hive of industry, and it was possibly his canny instinct which saw to it that Baron's Pride was limited to 90 or 100 mares a season, so that the horse lived actively to 22 years of age.

As exporters Montgomery did enormous trade, often having special trains standing at the local station, with up to 80 horses on each of them. Seemingly there were busy times when every available local youth was pressed into helping to get them there, and since trains left usually at about 4 am by all accounts there were some lively times at that station. Nor was it all one-way trade, and there was an occasion in 1896 when six horses came in from Colonel Holloway's American stud – five by Cedric incidentally. The Royal appointment could have gone up, by the way, with Queen Victoria's Osborne stock being headed by Baron Bombie, son of Baron's Pride.

William Montgomery retired in 1918, his partner having died six years previously and been succeeded by his nephew, also named Andrew. All 25 entire horses of three years and up were sold to average a handsome £557, with Drexel (16548) at eight years old, making 1,550gns. Special trains brought 4,000 people to that sale, so it must have been quite an event. An interesting comment on Andrew Montgomery's ideas on type is a recollection that at one major show he was judging and helped to put the Lord Lyon tribe down not a step but a whole stair – with all their fancy hair. Nephew 'Drew' set about re-establishing the stud, and in 1920 bought what was said to be the best two-year-old colt in the country, Fyvie Sensation (20042). Interestingly he was by Hiawatha Again (18765) out of a Footprint mare – in other words an outcross mix of Hiawatha and Baron's Pride strains. He was apparently not cheap either, but soon to reward his owner with the Highland Show championship, and the following spring the Cawdor Cup, when stud fees of £25 + £35 were asked. Scott Skinner, the legendary Scots' fiddler, seemingly wanted to compose a strathspey tune about the horse, so the romantic era was not done. Nor was it for the owner as it happens, since quite soon he decided to sell up and move out to the United States to be married.

There is an interesting postscript in that among the mares put to Fyvie Sensation was William Meiklem's Maud of Begg by Footprint. She bore a foal in 1922; it was named Benefactor, and in due course went to Netherhall. This was the stallion which was to make 4,400gns as a three-year-old to T. and M. Templeton of Sandyknowe when Montgomery dispersed, and James Kilpatrick was under-bidder. The horse won the Highland at Kelso 1926 when the stud also had the female award with Monk Gladys. A son of Benefactor who made his mark as sire, although not in the show ring, was Benedictine. He bred six Cawdor Cup winners and at 20 years was still leading sire.

Meiklem made a huge contribution to the Clydesdale's world, being a generous donor of trophies and breed society president. The name very nearly made breed history in a different way too – by providing the first woman president, for his wife followed the interest on her Arran estate; she was daughter of the Duke of Hamilton and it was often thought she would accept the office.

Matthew Marshall's fame can be attributed to Hiawatha, but his company farmed 1,800 acres in Wigtownshire, and at times the horse stock was as high as 300 head. That may seem to be a breathtaking figure, but several sources recalled seeing as many as 75 mares with foals on the place. Bridgebank Stud was dispersed in 1934, averaging £123.

The Aberdeenshire Sleighs were always prominent in Clydesdale circles. In 1926 Alexander Sleigh married Kilpatrick's daughter Peggy. It was said that John P. Sleigh of St John's Wells bred, owned or exhibited more Cawdor Cup winners than anyone else. In 1929 he certainly had three of them, with Wells Lady Ray, her daughter Ray Sun and Wells Lorna. Kismet (18417) was stud sire, classically bred by Footprint out of a Baron's Pride mare. Dunlop once offered £5,000 for the stallion, and when refused he simply turned away and went off to the station without a word. On another occasion John Sleigh was involved in a £900 deal with him for a 10-day-old filly foal. Dunlop wired that it was dying of strangles and the deal was off. Sleigh's reply by return was that it was still on, dead or alive! J. P. Sleigh was probably the first breeder ever to judge abroad – that was in 1927, though James Picken was not long behind him.

Sleigh's son Harry has in recent years been acknowledged master of Shetland ponies, owing much to his background no doubt. In his view the famous stud grooms deserved more praise than they ever received in the heyday of the horse. He named Johnny Coubray of Harviestoun, James Morgan of St Johns, and Fleming of Craigie Mains, plus McNight who worked with Montgomery. The only groom who ever got a fortune, according to the author's researches, was one called Staddon who in 1901 suddenly found he had inherited £75,000 from an uncle in Pittsburgh.

Lord Cawdor's stud at Nairn was influential in the north and he also kept horses at Stackpole Court in Wales. But the farthest outpost was that of Noss Stud near Wick where William Clyne bred good stock. On one occasion at least it was reported – in 1917 – that those attending his draught sale were required to go to local police offices for passports to travel beyond Inverness – presumably a wartime restriction.

Clydesdale interest extended to outer isles too. Over in Orkney there was sound stock and Shearer of Holm won the gelding championship at the national show with an entry in 1925, whilst Corrigan of North Bigging bred a horse that won locally and in the States. James Clark must have held the islander record though, for his mare Miss Oyama which took the Islay award for 14 years.

In the north of England R. Brydon's Seaham Harbour enterprise was a remarkable business, taking over the old Londonderry stud and on dispersal in 1916 they sold a hundred head to average £211. Top was Bonny Buchlyvie (14032) at 5,000gns to Kilpatrick. The famous grey stallion, Pearl Oyster (10831) was bred at the stud, tracing right back to Drew's Lucy.

Picken of Torrs Stud was a giant in the breed. Ambassador, which sold for 5,600gns at the Sandyknowe sale, was of his breeding and some said the horse was still the cheapest he ever produced, which was presumably why his tail was well plucked after the event for souvenirs. Torrs neighboured Craigie Mains when first founded.

The Kerr family of Wigton with Redhall stock went back to 1863, and once had the shocking experience of losing two top stallions within two hours of each other through ruptured blood vessels. They made top stock available at reasonable fees over a wide area and this was of inestimable value to the Clydesdale. John Kerr was breed president in 1948 and kept the showing record up too.

One wonders sometimes if those with an eye for a horse did not at times achieve as much honour as those who bred them. This was the case, for example, with William Taylor of Park Mains, discoverer of the stallion Sir Everard a full century ago. At the time the horse was a roughish yearling and cost £65, but many were to say in later years that this find redeemed the breed from the penalties of over-exploiting Prince of Wales and Darnley blood. Taylor's stock was sold in 1911 – he had 54 averaging £131. Near neighbour Walter Park of Hatton had a Top Gallant son amongst many good ones.

Misfortunes were many amongst Clydesdales, chiefly due to grass sickness, which robbed studs of their best stock at frequent intervals. Sandilands stud was one to miss real fame for it was well established by James Weir and son-in-law T. Purdie-Sommerville, led by Kerr's good stallion Scotland Yet. They had a bad fire in stables in 1925 losing eleven stallions and both partners died in 1930.

Enthusiasm ran in families. A good example was William Clark of Netherlea, who owned Royal Gartly and whose Baron's Best actually beat Baron of Buchlyvie in the showyard. Clark had five sons and four followed him into working with horses. Tom of Muirtons won his first Highland award in 1919, with Rising Star bred at St John's Wells. On a great occasion in Manchester for the Royal Show of England, this breeder brought out 29 geldings – and won against Shires. Muirton horses continued the progress with four Cawdor Cups between 1943 and 1955. The Windlaw prefix to which the youngest son James succeeded continued to win honours, and in his son's time as well. Alexander McCormick worked there as groom for 35 years, bringing out four Meiklem Gold Cup winners. Clark had a big gelding trade with contracts for the railway companies and other large users, and it was Sandy who bought most of them in for him. It was said that he never knew anything about an eight hour day and at shows seldom, if ever, left his charges.

A stud formed in 1897 was Johnston, owned by R. and J. Chapman. In the '20s it consisted of 12 mares and as many stallions, including Dupplin Castle (20747) bred by Lord Forteviot. Robert Chapman had been a leading dog-fancier, taking up horses late in life and by trade he was a licensee. It was in the 1950s that a descendant brought the stud name to prominence in a very lean time for Clydes with £2 plus £6 set for stud fees.

Continuity can be noted also in the family of Murdoch of Balgreen, who provided the centenary year president. Henry Murdoch's Balgreen Final Command (24094) was a notable stallion of modern times, said to have been the only yearling ever to be supreme at the Stallion show. It was largely his influence which took the breed into its second century on a dominant note.

Seven

Prizes and Premium Prices

Modern farming began its course of improvement in the 1830s, which is when machinery and the use of fertilizers came to be closely associated with general husbandry systems. Alongside these was a wish to improve the standards of stock performance, and an awareness that in some districts superior quality strains existed which gave better performance than the norm. This applied especially to horses, which were objects of special pride and interest, as well as being manifestly the tractive power. Accordingly there were moves to establish premiums for those likely to improve the stock, and from these developed the competitive show as the means of both selecting superior specimens and letting them be seen publicly. The show gave scientific stockbreeding an incentive to improvement, and although it has often been criticized it has never been bettered.

The major fault with breeders who have had show-ring excellence as their aim has always been a tendency to over-exaggerate on points of perfection. For this reason heavy horse users have sounded a clarion call to breeders which has sometimes even been heeded: 'Keep the lorry in view'. A sensible slogan in fact, because particularly in the early days the Clydesdale's most vital attribute was its very characteristic and lively step allied to great strength and wearing qualities. There has always been acceptance that good bone was a basis of soundness and – reluctantly perhaps – that extremes could endanger trade. Certainly such thoughts would have been paramount when in the early days of showing there were perhaps 50 or more cart geldings in a line, and the sire of the winner would be given a rating for life on the result.

No prize arena anywhere can match that of the Clydesdale horse for competitiveness, and the anecdote of the peer remarking to another who was highly successful on the Turf that he'd rather win a first-prize ticket on Glasgow Green than at the Derby or the Oaks, is not exaggerated. That is how people felt, and enthusiasm has not one whit diminished with the passage of time and its mechanical changes.

A report issued in 1887 puts showing well in perspective thus: 'We can confidently affirm that an immense improvement amongst our young stock may be dated from the time we began to have prize stallions in our district; also that foreigners and their agents in search of young Clydesdales for export are attracted to the district as a result.'

There was actually a great community pride in the stallion selected to cover the district's mares; especially should it be a top show animal or aristocrat of the breed. Landowners on their part went to great pains (and expense) to procure good types of horses, knowing very well that improvement in husbandry followed and that it was a sound investment and made a good image too.

The most brilliant Clydesdale parades were always at the Highland Show, particularly in the mid-1860s, the formative years of the breed when the parading of outstanding horses created enormous interest. It was much as is occasioned today by a completely new model of motor-car. Imagine the talk in remote villages over events such as the national show in Dumfries, 1870, when Peter Crawford's Rantin' Robin beat the great horse Prince of Wales. The horse thereafter travelled all over the Border country before being exported to Australia. One suspects too that there was many a bet on the outcome of championships, as for example in 1877 when Darnley was supreme stallion; but the money was on the chances of Weir's Prince George Frederick beating Drew's Lord Harry. Alas the challenger never materialized and Weir well recouped the 500gns he paid for his horse as a yearling.

Some indication of the landlords' investment in improving stallions is provided by the £400 allowance the Earl of Tankerville paid for a season, having hired Riddell's Baron Keir for his tenants' use in Chillingham, Norfolk.

A revealing glimpse of breed rivalries and attitudes comes from an account of the Yorkshire Society's show in Bradford 1890, when the trio of judges was composed of two Shire and one Clydesdale experts. Both the senior Clydesdale stallions exhibited were placed, whereupon a steward told the judges they had been declared unsound and must be withdrawn. Independent veterinary surgeons later refuted the decision and long afterwards the legs were sent away for dissection and the fault never found. More jealousy was claimed at the Royal Show in 1896 when the champion Clyde was Prince Sturdy but it was said that the breed was hurried out of view, whilst Shires were given a chance to display their paces. When Lord Londonderry's Walter out of a Darnley mare was champion agricultural gelding, and beat the Shire champion, it was a night of rejoicing, and the fact that the horse had rival blood in its veins on both sides of its breeding was overlooked.

Much of this show-ring niggling was petty stuff, but does serve to illustrate how much these events were valued as exhibitions, and the means to attract interest and stimulate sales abroad: none better either than the great event at Crystal Palace in 1897 to honour Queen Victoria's Diamond Jubilee. There was a parade of 15 different horse breeds that existed in the United Kingdom, and Clydesdales were represented by the stallion Briarwood (10038) and Montrave Crown Imperial – both from Lords Arthur and Cecil. And the same year Higgins' team of three Clydes and a Shire won the London Cart-horse Parade.

There is no doubt that the Cawdor Cup contests contributed much to showyard interest and stimulated improvement. The first was in 1892 when William Renwick's Prince Alexander won from Prince Robert and both were sons of Prince of Wales. Incidentally it took six judges and an umpire's vote to decide it.

Without shows it is doubtful if Baron's Pride progeny would ever have gained the startling recognition that was their due. The turn of the century brought their qualities before the public and they soon dominated competition. When Mr Wood's B. Pride colt came from Pontefract to win the Highland Show supreme award he was only the second yearling ever to achieve it. At show after show almost every winner could be attributed to the same sire – a notable exception being in 1905 when W. S. Park's Royal Chattan beat Baron of Buchlyvie, but then the dam was by B. Pride.

With such dominance it is surprising, possibly, that show-ring interest was so intense at this period. At that particular event the champions attracted such a crowd that mounted policemen had to clear a way for them and the ropes around the ring gave way under the press of people. The fact that in 1906 a breeder should take a case to court over show rules is a further indication of the way feelings developed.

The year 1909 could be taken as the zenith of Baron's Pride's success in the show-ring, when J. E. Kerr's Nerissa was female champion at the national event, J. P. Sleigh's Moira was Cawdor Cup winner, the Montgomerys' Fyvie Baron was male champion and Dunure Footprint was a reserve champion although the yearling sensation of the season. Every first prize-winner in all classes owed descent to Baron's Pride and this was long talked about and studied by geneticists.

Having conveyed the impression of intense competition in show-rings it is only fair to point to the strain under which judges carried out their heavy tasks. Complaints were very common as may be supposed. Consider for example the show at which three judges officiated and in one class was a mare bred by one, owned up to recent weeks by another, and the third did not like her. After one national show in 1900 it was recorded: 'A small percentage of the animals were considered rightly placed . . .'. No doubt McNeilage was behind that remark. Matters came to a head in 1906 at a breed society meeting when it was claimed that attempts were being made to influence judges by disclosures of owner- ship. A progressive step was taken by instituting a ballot for selection to the panel of judges.

That there were some straightforward exhibitors, undaunted by fashion trends, is proved by the success of one James Stewart who in winning first prize at Buchlyvie Show with a black filly foal exactly repeated the achievement of his father 44 years earlier. And in that time the family had never missed a show; moreover the winning animal went back to the first over several generations. Such is the real unchanging and undaunted backbone of any breed of stock.

It was the end of an era in 1912 when Baron's Pride died 'of no illness at all' and he had been top sire from 1895 without being challenged. His equally illustrious son, Baron of Buchlyvie, was just as dominant, as may be illustrated by 28 progeny at eight shows securing 61 prizes. Over the next decade it was only in one year that honours went other than to this line of breeding. When Robert Brydon of Seaham Harbour gave a massive silver shield to be contested for by champion stallions, he anticipated it would be a perpetual award for a lifetime because successive wins were undreamed of, and yet Kilpatrick won it twice and largely due to the Baron's outstanding quality. He supplied a replace- ment and it bore tribute to the horse in a silver replica.

The Great War obviously disrupted showing and the recession which followed did not help either. But the '20s produced huge classes of horses and the London Cart Horse Society, for example, could draw 519 out for a parade, whilst Glasgow could show 138 horses in a street display. It was quite a triumph then in 1920 for M. J. Dunlop and Co. of Clyde Ironworks when they won a gold medal with a cart horse aged 21 years – for 16 years the gelding had been in the care of James Barr who proudly won five times with his charge. That says much for the interest of the men who drove horses in those dreary times.

Breed society membership actually reached a peak of 3,930 in 1922 and there was no increase until 1935 when 70 newcomers were admitted. That was the year when a £100 subsidy was offered to teams of Clydes- dales going to the Royal Show to demonstrate their prowess. Dorman Long took up the offer and their whip James Mason must have looked smart in white overalls and white top hat. They won too, and it is an indication of the team's strength that they were walked 25 miles to the show pulling a load of over two tons.

The preparation of horses for show has been an art handed on from father to son, and still in these sophisticated days goes on. A lecturer in

Above: A long line in the decorated harness show class

Left: Close-up of the magnificent decorated show harness showing floral patterns on the saddle

Above: Early harness. The plaited horse collar from the Outer Hebrides is a rare example

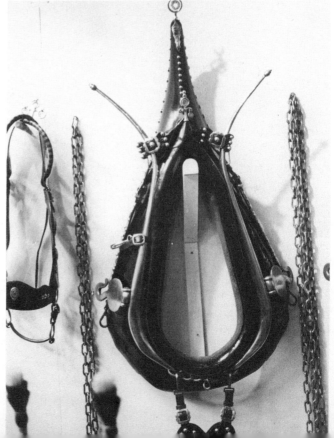

Right: A Clydesdale pattern collar and hames

Above: Robert Woods, Chief Carter, with James Buchanan and Co's winning gelding Chester, in Clydesdale tack

Below: Buchanan horses demonstrate the harness hitch

The six-horse hitch in action – and how well they move!

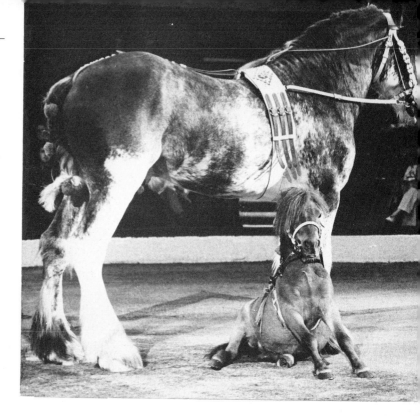

Right: Circus duo –
Clydesdale and
Shetland pony

Below: Champion female Hayston Alanna

Above: A champion gelding from Blackbyres at Scotstoun, 1947

Below: A foal champion from Craigie Mains, 1946

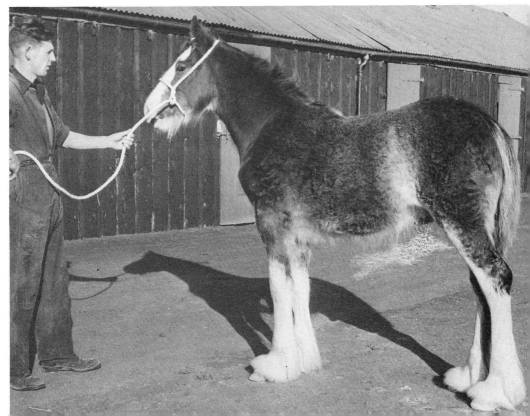

Clydesdales return to Aberdeen city streets. The team has joined the city council parks department because costings showed horses to be cheaper than motor transport

earlier years recalled that in 1883 he had seen a class of 50 colts shown naturally, but then they had taken to trying to make Clydesdales what they were not. All one heard about, he complained, was leash (straight hair) and spats, as though there was nothing more beautiful to a good horse and yet so far as utility was concerned it served no purpose. He thought judges could not see the real horses because they were hidden under blankets of flesh and plated for six months to draw out the feet and enable an exhibitor to put on an abnormal-sized shoe, or canted behind by an expert blacksmith so as to walk closely behind. Interesting observations, but it must be accepted that it is never wrong to try and present a competition entry in best form.

The next period of domination belonged entirely to James Kilpatrick and many wondered if the very magic of the name did not influence judges. A. N. M. Buchanan wrote: '. . . he may perhaps have had more than his fair share on many occasions, he certainly won many times with horses which in other hands had been unsuccessful, and also with horses which afterwards in other ownership could not get to the top . . . but then he was, of course, a master at bringing them out and showing.'

Official recognition of the draught horse by government ended in 1957 when grants were withdrawn, but this was not the mortal blow that many predicted. Shows still boasted entries not so far below those of 20 years previously. And now the real enthusiasts were taking over, following a hobby rather than a business, albeit a profitable one.

It was somehow right that the centenary stallion show at Scotstoun, in 1961, scene of so many triumphs for his family, should see Allan Kilpatrick win with Craigie Gallant Hero, and take another Cawdor Cup outright to make it the fourth claimed by the famous stud. To be accurate about dates was impossible. There was evidence of such an event as far back as 1844, and Glasgow Agricultural Society, as organizers, came into being in 1857; but even so the first-ever stallion show was in Edinburgh in 1756 when a £10 premium was offered.

There was another notable success in the '60s, when in 1964 James C. Picken's Torrs Renown was show champion. Remarkably, this honour had eluded the family in the past – three generations had been showing – and even then it was on an umpire's decision.

The Clydesdale Horse Society's centenary year in 1977 was marked by an upsurge in interest and fittingly out of 86 horses the best was from the president, William Murdoch, whose ten-month-old filly Balgreen Dollar Princess was by Doura Excelsior, a sire that had gone to Canada. He had been in the ownership of John Young of Girvan Mains, a name synonymous with the modern Clydesdales, so it was interesting that his son, J. W. Young, should win the Cawdor with a son of the same sire. The generations came close in horses and men, as

65

for instance when the Thomas Clark Memorial Trophy was won by T. Clark and Son's Muirton Sceptre. Later at the summer show the female Cawdor Cup went to Kettlestoun Lucinda (R. Lawrie) and leading exporter of the day, Peter M. Sharp, brought out the male winner with Bardrill Bell Ringer that will doubtless be flying the flag abroad.

So in a century of improvement incredibly things stay much the same, and that is the real secret of success: like perpetuating like all down the generations. In all these years the Clydesdale has worked, educated, and entertained. It has enjoyed a huge public and fascinated scientists as well as politicians. Those who unequivocally predicted its demise have succeeded only in seeing it come round full circle and back to strength again.

Closely allied to showing is the selling of horses and if a graph of average prices were to be drawn, they would reflect the economic state of the country as a whole. What is also certain is that good horses have always been highly valued, and of course the four-figure prices of earlier times could be equated now in terms of a quarter or half million pounds.

Socially it is interesting that the important horse fair and hiring days which involved high levels of dealings in stock and transfer of labour, are now completely gone and have been replaced by private dealing and engagements. It is doubted if either event will be missed.

It is useful, however, to have on record the cost of working Clydesdales in the nineteenth century. That one Thomas Brown, a Teviotdale farmer, should have travelled to Rutherglen Fair and paid £45 apiece for four-year-old geldings, is an indication that prices were high and good work horses for draught clearly at a premium. He also bought a carriage Cleveland at the same time and it made one of a work pair with a Clyde and by his testimony 'wrought six days a week and drove to church on Sunday'.

By 1879 farmers were paying as much as £250 for a pair of horses, which means values more than doubled inside a quarter century. The rise was occasioned by shortage, due to severe losses in several wet years and extra heavy labour and very heavy export sales. In fact horses became so scarce that it was even felt that farmers should return to using oxen. No wonder stallions were engaged at up to £100 premiums long before the start of normal hirings, and most had over 80 mares guaranteed at £4, equal to some £500 for a season. French and German agents were attending the fairs and taking up to 300 horses at a time back with them.

When in 1876 a farmer had to pay takeover for a new holding which averaged £105 9s for 11 horses, they were approaching sensational values. No wonder the tramway company imported 18 horses from America –

in Texas native stock was £5 a head.

After the peak came the trough, as for example when in 1880 a year-ling colt made only 13gns and that was a good one. On the other hand the Duke of Buccleuch paid £110 for a gelding from Muncraig, which was considered remarkable and the price of outstanding merit.

The ups and downs of trade can be seen in reports for 1896 when foals at Perth averaged £4, geldings sold at £50, and Lord Londonderry's fine horses averaged £41 – at a time when drafts of Shire horses were over £117. Sir John Stirling Maxwell's Clydes averaged £67 and Sir Walter Gilbey's Shires from Elsenham £143 – the Shire always had fashionable patrons even in hard times. But still these prices are all much better than two years previously when Craigie House Stud sold 23 horses for a *total* of £543 or £26 11s 3d average. Even the auctioneer went on record as saying they had been thrown away.

Some idea of the pattern of trade at this period is seen in reports of hundreds of strong geldings being sold into London, Newcastle and other major cities for draught work. A dozen dealers operated in Carlisle to pick up Cumbrian and Border heavy horses. One example scaled 19¼cwt in thin condition and stood 17 hands high, made £75 at auction, resold to a dealer for £85 and then to a London buyer at £120.

Commercially there were big sales at the turn of the century when tramcar horses were displaced by electric vehicles. It was said that a thousand cars made 10,000 horses redundant in Britain. The average price was low with £15 to £24 quoted. One farmer who bought a tram-way horse found that it would only start to move if he rang a bell!

Seaham Harbour sale in 1915 was a major one with 100 horses at £212 average. Kilpatrick recalled paying 5,000gns for Bonnie Buchlyvie there, although actually it was pounds because the auctioneer made a slip in the bidding and the shrewd horse breeder noted it and put his cash down. That year 85 Canadian-bred Clydesdales were sold in Glasgow with three-year-old colts 54–68gns, 5–6-year-olds 68–100gns. There was also a batch of 64 from A. and E. Aguirre's *estancia* in the Argentine sent back home too. These imports set against only 250 exports make an interesting comparison.

After World War I record prices were paid everywhere. These were for geldings sold at £200 and W. Yates of Appleby paid a record 1,850gns in 1918 for a mare Dunure Glad Eye, whilst in the following year Mrs Kinloch of Cardross got £3,400 for a yearling colt by Prince Ossian. Opportune dispersals included A. and W. Montgomery's, averaging £557, and Dickens and Butlers' at £400. Lanark's great sales lasted six days and drew 3,000 people to the ringsides.

After such heady prices it must have been disappointing to get a down-turn by 1921. One market report stated: 'Three not unsound horses were sold by auction at £17, £3 and £2, average £7 6s 8d'. George Clyne's Noss Stud sold up for £51 average. Stallion men were gloomily contemplating losses on terms of £1 10s + £3 and one with 20 horses on the road complained that only three were breaking even.

By the '30s Clydesdales were up in strength and horse breeding was one of the brighter spots in the agricultural depression, which seems paradoxical but was occasioned by shortage. Lanark celebrated its 50th year with four days and an entry of 1,195 horses. Belgian and Canadian imports were a feature of the period, but still good geldings made up to £150 and continued to do so right up to the eve of World War II.

Just as in 1914 the outbreak of war sent values soaring, which is the more surprising if we consider the completely different role allotted the horse. Geldings averaged £109 at leading sales and went as high as £360; by 1945 there was report of an 18 hands-high cart gelding making £500 and a pair from Irving Holliday, a most successful exhibitor, brought £610.

That was the turn of the tide, however; a world at peace saw no immediate use for draught horses and they were going to the knackers. Stallions still travelling met no demand and at the main centres trade fell back almost exactly to levels of 1940, when an average of only £27 was struck. But the fact that a city corporation was able to parade 80 geldings in a show was evidence that horses were still at work.

The Clydesdale Society AGM was told ominously by its president, John Kerr, that many promising young horses were finding their way to processing machines instead of to the plough. Then as often happened earlier shortage started to creep back and by the end of the decade more mares were being bred and sale averages had bounced up £10 a head.

The '50s proved a surprise to everyone for the heavy horses climbed back from the brink. Lanark returned an £88 average for 77 geldings, going up to £200. W. R. S. Young and Sons got a post-war record of £550 for a colt foal from Muirtons – it was bred from their top sire M. Monarch. Perhaps it was an earnest appeal from Hugh McGregor that was heeded. This popular horseman and former exporter urged that the time had come to stand up for the draught Clydesdale when it had its back to the wall. He quoted the alarming spread of grass sickness, started amongst a camp of army horses in Angus in 1908, and now continually recurring. Characteristically he added: 'Where many a whistling contented ploughman had tied up tails on Spring morning, the box was now needed for battery hens. We in Scotland built up horse breeding societies to make the Clydesdale stallion available at practically every farm, and now it is all going.'

He was right in that last respect, for local societies were amalgamating to try and make a season for one horse. His own district of Doune, once a great nursery for the breed, had 20 mares covered in 1956 where 15 years earlier there had been 500. Returns showed young stock down a third and falling dangerously near to 40,000 horses overall.

If statistically the heavy horse had ceased to count, then there was a welcome upturn to trade. John Strang's mare Princess sold at Wigton in 1978 for 3,400gns, and her filly foal made 1,300gns. Four figures became a general level rather than the exception and it continues to be the case. So if trade be the barometer of health then the Clydesdale is in very fit state. Show and sale rings are thronged again, and as in all the times before the best continue to go overseas.

Eight

The Ambassadors

The outstanding achievement of the Clydesdale horse was the contribution it made to world agriculture between the latter end of the nineteenth and the early twentieth centuries. In this period vast numbers were shipped with trading at a very high level, and the breeding stock was used to up-grade native stocks and to impart much improved draught horse power. In opening up the vast prairie landscapes to corn production the horses performed a gigantic task; equally significant was the contribution to haulage work in the cities. They have scarcely been given the credit that is their due for these labours.

Much of the trade that took place was in top quality horses for breeding purposes, because of the very high shipping costs. Specialists would make purchases in the home country on a speculative basis, telegraphing ahead to prospective buyers to meet the shipments at the docks. The largest breeders virtually established branches out in the new territories, and they frequently sent out stallions to hire for the season. More than a few actually set up farming units in the New World, becoming very prosperous too.

It has been said that it was in the late nineteenth century that Clydesdales lost the Middle West of America markets, and that after World War I the breed was put on trial in north-west Canada in competition with the Percheron. Statistics that are available show a steady increase in exports from about 500 in the early 1880s to well over 1,000 head, then in the following decade the trade fell back. The new century opened with only 178 horses sold abroad, climbing to 1,600 head within ten years.

Whilst Canada and the USA were the major markets, Australian trade was brisk enough, and the Clydesdale made a good contribution in that country, as also in New Zealand where it had many supporters. Russia bought breeding stock in most years, as did South Africa and

Argentina, whilst the Continental trade was frequently brisk and was two-way in that if home markets were active dealers were wont to ship strong horses back and forth across the Channel.

That there were major scandals in the export business during boom spells is perfectly obvious. There were countless examples of unscrupulous dealings and exploitation, and in the long term it caused much vexation and dismay because it cost support when it was most needed. The Select Clydesdale Book secretary on one occasion said that men stood condemned who had sent non-prolific horses overseas. They sent those that would or could not breed, those not true to type, and those of uncertain pedigree – invariably describing these as 'Baron's Prides' or 'after Footprint' or as the fashionable line of the day. It was a shameless business and few were completely innocent.

There is another side to the story: demand was such that prospective buyers worldwide were desperate for horses, irrespective of breed or character, and in their greed they scarcely cared about the details. In 1887 a Royal Commission for the encouragement of horse breeding reported: 'It is a matter of common notoriety that year after year the United Kingdom has been swept by the agents of foreign governments for the stallions and mares best suited to the purposes . . . this country has been left with the inferior and often unsound animals which the foreign agents have rejected.' So it did work both ways, possibly even to the extent that all home breeders had left to sell abroad were those previously rejected; certainly many of the best went abroad when they could ill be spared. It happens still . . .

Overseas horsemen were very critical, frequently voicing dissatisfaction with draught horses incapable of drawing to capacity – possibly they expected too much. But they were readier with praise for Clydesdales as being the most likely to perform, sound in feet and limb and with good straight action or movement. They scoffed at breeders' mania for fancy show points, perhaps without fully understanding that the commercial result was producing what they sought.

The drain on horse-breeding is reflected in reports of the period 1883–9 when around 1,000 stallions were being shipped annually. Many were lost in transit, although it was a matter of some pride that Clydesdales tended to be superior travellers.

A Clydesdale Breeders' Association of the United States was formed in 1879, just a year after publication of the first stud book in Britain. It was a time of rapid expansion in American agriculture – hence the need for horses and power. Pioneers are generally considered to have been Powell Brothers of Springboro, Pennsylvania; N. P. Clarke, St Cloud, Minnesota; Robert Holloway, Alexis, Illinois; Galbraith Brothers, Janesville, Wisconsin; and Brookside Farm, Fort Wayne,

Indiana.

One of the earliest horses to have made an impression seems to have been Donald Dinnie, bred in the north-east by G. Alexander of Bourtie, sent out to R. Thompson in east Missouri. Holloway was first president of the American society and bought four stallions that year, amongst which was the Duke of Portland's Cairnbrogie Keir that went on to win handsomely, including the Grand Sweepstake in Chicago 1883 – oddly enough being sold back to the Duke for £1,400 and winning back home at the Royal Show.

Colonel Holloway was a colourful man, a barrister, and super-enthusiast involved in all manner of enterprises but never doing today what could be done tomorrow. A native of Kentucky, he had adventures in the civil war and died in 1906. His stud sale in 1899 saw 51 horses average £100 and seven were bought for Scotland. The Montgomerys were regular buyers, particularly of the stallion Cedric's stock, to sell back home. At one time Holloway had a large acreage, including a stud based in the Western prairie lands. One possible reason why he was not always very popular was his alliance with an organization known as the 'Glasgow Horse Breeding and Exporting Co.' which was often in dispute over various matters. On one occasion the US Court ordered him to dis-pose of Clydesdales belonging to him. In one instance of 52 horses represented as his property in a sale catalogue, the Company alleged that only seven were his and that he owed them half a million dollars. Compromise settled a protracted dispute, but it was not an isolated case. The Company obviously operated on a fair scale, because in 1883 they bought 600 acres in Iowa as headquarters, with mention of having brood mares in the stud.

Holloway was pretty aggressive with his promotions for the breed too. Not content with taking the best horses he also made a bid for the parent society's popular secretary Archie McNeilage. The outcome was a salary rise to stay where he was.

Alex Galbraith seems to have been one of the best imports into the States. Born in Killearn, he went out to Janesville and soon became 'Dean of draught horse judges' – possibly because he was honoured by the University of his adopted State in 1911. He bred a notable stallion in Johnny Cope (416) by Justice, that won at the Highland Show in 1857 and bred Campsie and Young Campsie – the latter being sold by Riddell to the Emperor of Austria.

The Galbraiths were major exhibitors at Chicago and Minnesota fairs, notably with Prince George of Wales who helped the breed make its mark. Initially at least they appear to have maintained the home stud of Croy-Cunningham in Stirlingshire that was founded in 1835, and used the American farms as a depot. The stallion George Buchanan (329) was said to have been the third to be imported into the States.

Numerous Scots followed this pattern, including Alex Mitchell who in 1882 took a yearling colt to his Iowa farm from Fyvie. Operating from their US base the Caia Brothers of Arlington Heights also had a place in Annan, Dumfries, becoming one of the largest importers to America.

As trade developed so, of course, problems multiplied and the American breed society did all it could to tighten up on pedigrees, banning odd colours, and generally showing dealers they would not accept any old horse. And once trade became two-way the parent body began to get tougher on registrations. Court cases and disputes over pedigrees were not lacking and the Clydesdale Society often had to send officials over to act as expert witnesses.

Mr W. G. Powell of Springboro, an early president of the American association, summed up Clydesdale qualities as surpassing all others in the ability to keep up the strain of draught work. It was a nice testimony. He added that the Clydesdale had more reserves, as well as greater prepotency in breeding, when crossed with ordinary stock in the States.

A good specimen surely, widely exhibited in 1889, was a five-year-old, who weighed nearly 3,000lb, stood 20¾ hands high, 32in. round the arm, 45in. around the stifle, with a 7ft 11in. girth, 34½in. round the hip, 11ft. 4in. in length, with a head 36in. long and had shoes weighing 32lb.

The boom years lasted to the later 1890s when Alex Galbraith, who was breed secretary, reported that depression was affecting trade, there was a craze for bicycles and more electric street cars were being used. Horses sold by weight made the best returns. In bankruptcy reports losses on horse shipments were frequently being cited, as also depreciation in values of Clydesdale stallions compared with the original cost. By 1900 the Canadian and American breed associations had discussed merging.

With good reason the Americans always insisted on performance in their horses, with ample weight and conformation simply assessed as being as wide as a wagon with a leg at each corner. One good report was from a Kansas farmer who had four Clydesdale mares, two teams of mules, four Percheron mares, and some Percheron × Belgians. One Clyde mare died in foaling and two others sold well, leaving one for which there were no takers. In the ten months during which the owner was trying to sell her this mare killed a Percheron 200lb heavier by walking her to death, wore another mare down 400lb in weight and was reported to be doing singly what a team of good mules was called on to do in one spring. It was pointed out that the owner did not credit the Clydesdale mare with the work done; instead he charged a dead

Percheron, another run-down, and a team of loafing mules against her!

For performance, Robert Ogilvie, American breed secretary in 1911, had a good representative in the stallion MacQueen (5200), which had died aged 26 years, having beaten everything in Chicago and Toronto, and been sold to Graham Brothers in Canada. In eight seasons he served 1,718 mares and had 1,079 foals – and was active to the end.

The real test that developed, however, was in pulling and team contests which were unique to the States. Clydesdales bought through Netherhall won the six-horse teams at Chicago in 1907, despite money without stint seemingly being spent on the rival Percherons for a win. At about this time Beckton Stock Farms, Wyoming, were taking a team of 18 horses around the Fairs, often in round trips of over 3,000 miles. It took determination in those days. Such determination was shown by Peter Walker and Sons, Liverpool brewers, who took out a team to Chicago and caused a sensation with them, despite the fact that half of them never even got there due to a rough passage. The remainder won a gold medal and were brought home again. The 'hitch' horses at these events would be shown singly, and then usually in teams of two, four and six to a wagon. When not on the show circuit they would be at work in city streets and the practice continues today with their advertising value much esteemed. The value of such teams was stressed back in 1930 by the Ice Cream Trade Journal of New York which summed up manufacturers' publicity plans. Ross and Moore pointed out how people were interested in their horses, and thus they attracted attention to the exhibit. Since the horses were in regular work for nine months only three months were a charge against the profits.

Six-horse hitches were introduced in the show rings of Chicago in 1900 and have been a regular feature ever since. For some reason they never caught on in the UK or Europe to the same extent, although in 1909 a draught team sent over by Morris and Company caused a sensation at the main shows. The wheelers were both home-bred and the whip, John Hamilton, drove them through figures-of-eight and turned the leaders on the gallop.

The most famous whip was Billy Wales, who drove a team for the Chicago Stockyard Company, and in mid-20s to '30s won against all-comers on the North American continent. His horses weighed a ton apiece and Billy had his hands insured for $50,000. He was not exclusively a Clydesdale handler but had a super Clyde, Sir Hubert, that was a Grand Champion and was said to have been the most photographed horse in America, even having his painting done in oils for the Saddle and Sirloin Club Gallery.

In recent times the most notable teams have been those of the Anheuser Busch Company, successfully publicizing Budweiser beers with six and eight horse hitches. Irving Holliday and Peter N. Sharp have often been responsible for matching them up, but the brewers have a large stud and their president August A. Busch has been generous in making stallions available free of charge.

Ed Clausen of Gladbrook, Iowa, is another hitching expert and his six-horse all-black Clydesdales have been expertly shown. That they are still an attraction is evident from his grand-daughter Becky Thoms' message to me that a lot of people beginning in the draught horse world are starting to show, aiming at six-horse hitches.

Don Castagnasso and Sons of Charlotte, who have exported to the homeland, run a winning six-hitch, as also do the Lewis Ranch in Lincoln who have shown teams of eight in Kansas, Colorado, Iowa and Nebraska. Ed Henken of Ferndale is another enthusiast with a big, weighty team and many champion mares besides.

Pulling tests of strength are another feature of competition in the States, which have not been tried elsewhere. In some trials hitches are tested against a dynamometer and it creates great public interest.

For a country so conscious of its mechanized state, it seems incredible that the American Clydesdale scene should be still so active. A draught horse workshop sponsored by the North Adams State College is specially run to help those interested in hitching and driving. It is but one example of a continuing enthusiasm.

The first Clydesdale import to Canada, in 1840, was the stallion Cumberland by Glenelg (356) that went to David Rowntree Jnr. of Weston, Ontario. The Canadian Stud Book's first volume appeared seemingly a long time afterwards in 1886 and included a grey Clyde by Young Clyde (949) that went out in 1842 and is generally regarded as having marked the start of Clydesdale history there. He won at Toronto 1846 and at one period 17 young stallions by this horse were in a parade and all were described as superior to local stock. The horse went on to the USA but died a year later in 1851. Until 1870 only three females had been taken into Canada but that first stud book recorded 74 imports.

'The Clydesdale made Canada draught-horse conscious and Canada owes it a lasting debt,' according to one tribute paid to the breed. Pioneers included Joe Thompson, native of Yorkshire, who went to Columbus, Ontario; he was said to have lost his horses several times on their shipments out, so returning home with only bridle and blankets for his outlay. Happily when down and out financially, neighbours subscribed to a fund to give him another chance and he imported Netherby, a horse which wiped out all his debts: a nice illustration of the tenacity and enthusiasm which gripped such men the world over.

Graham Brothers were also pioneers. They were importing from 1870 and one of their best was the stallion MacQueen. A note puts his stud earnings from 1898 to 1906 at $21,090.

Clydesdales had to compete with a strong challenge from Percherons in Canada. A report from Manitoba in 1884 gave numbers as 52 Clyde stallions against 35 Percheron, 23 French Canadian and 59 general-purpose types. By 1920 Percherons had gained the ground in America whilst Canada was two-thirds Clydesdale. M. Galbraith of Alberta put it as being 'neck and neck' in Western Canada, being critical of the fact that Clydesdales had lost ground through the sacrifice of weight and substance to what he contemptuously termed 'prettiness'. When, in the early '20s, the Alberta Government bought Craigie Masterpiece it was said the purpose was to stop Percheron progress.

By 1905 a heavy trade had built up across the Atlantic. The Montgomerys shipped 120 horses and also let 13 premium stallions to societies. Even better was the purchase back by William Montgomery of the stallion Benedict, as proof some said that excellent quality horses were being bred overseas. The same year Park's filly Rosadora became the first Cawdor Cup winner to be shipped – she went to W. H. Bryce, Arcola, Canada. At this period Thomas Mercer developed a keen interest, being one of a family with headquarters at Markdale, Ontario, for shipping the horses. It was big business by this time.

Toronto has always been one of the great exhibition centres in the world and it was significant that the 1902 Fair was the 25th arranged by the Clydesdale Association. It lasted three days and had a full house each night – and indeed it still does. It was reported then that the ladies turned out in their gayest gowns, and today it is still one of the very few world-class shows at which patrons wear evening dress; it remains immensely prestigious.

A spring stallion show was started and Glinns (3655), son of Druid, was the first senior winner. D. and O. Sorby of Guelph had a win with Grandeur (6814), son of Darnley, and at the 1896 Toronto Fair took champion and family group over all breeds. Jeffrey Brothers of Whitby, Ontario, achieved something similar with the stallion Windsor.

One of the best quality shipments of Clydesdales ever landed in Canada went just before World War I when J. E. Kerr's Cawdor Cup mare Nerissa went out at a high price, together with Peggy Pride and two from Stephen Mitchell. Saskatchewan University had a major stud and paid £3,000 for George Ferguson's Cawdor Cup mare Rosalind. The sale of four champions in a year was very much a loss to the home country and evidence that overseas buyers were prepared to pay up handsomely for the choicest stock.

There was interesting work proceeding at this time in Quebec where Dr M'Eachran of Ormstown was carrying out experimental crossing of

Clydes with Shires, on rather similar lines to that done earlier by Riddell and Drew. His objective was apparently to increase bulk, weight of bone, restore fertility and improve colourings. No great results materialized but the very fact that the attempt was made can be seen as indication of the need at the time. Possibly this is another reason why top quality stock was bought in.

Some idea of the draught performance sought on the Prairies in the '20s is given in the following examples of output. A seven-horse team to a three-furrow plough with roller or packer attached managed eight acres a day. A six-horse team cultivating with 12ft tackle achieved 30 acres, whilst a similar team to a 12ft drill of 24 runs with double disc sowed 25 acres. These rates were exceeded later in the season once the horses had got hardened to the work. Four horse teams were used on binders to cut corn (8ft cut), averaging 18 to 20 acres a day. These massive teams must have taken some handling, even on those wide open spaces. One account of work in southern Alberta mentioned ploughing with up to 12 horses in yoke. Later work in cultivators gave such a team a 30ft spread of tackle. They were even known to yoke the inside horses by their tails to save harness!

The Prince of Wales (Duke of Windsor) owned a ranch near Calgary where Clydesdales were bred, and created considerable interest too. Professor W. L. Carlyle appears to have supervised it and HRH insisted from the start that Clydesdales should be kept there, with the nucleus specially imported. They were shown successfully and in 1923 brought out Calgary's Grand Champion, a filly called Balcairn Ringlet by Dunure Refiner. A stallion was taken out especially to exhibit for the ranch at the Canadian National in 1929.

The examples of Clydesdales put into Canadian experimental farms had a profound effect on their wider use. There was the Central Farm in Ottawa for example, founded in 1915 by Dr E. S. Archibald with brood mares supplied. Sir James Calder gave the first stallion, Sandy Mac, in 1924, and after four seasons he was followed by Precedence. Then in the '30s a selection of five stallions was made in Scotland and these were put round the experimental farms. The best was stated to be Windlaw Gayman (21933), bred by John Telfer at Priestside. An outstanding mare was Darling of Begg, giving two filly and eight colt foals – her last was Lady Begg in 1923 when 14 years old and this daughter of High Grade had nine fillies in ten years to found a stock.

Robert and Albert Ness of Howick, Quebec, were active importers at this time and they remained so, also having a great Ayrshire dairy stock in later years. Ben Rothwell, Hillsdale, Ottawa, showed the stallion Brunstane Zenith (21555). He was an importer of stock over 60 years, and this was his best one. Although 85 years old he showed the horse himself and took Grand Champion at Toronto, Central Canada and Ottawa shows.

The later '30s brought a fall and one news report stated that by 1936 in the Canadian Prairies, some 677,192 horses had been displaced through mechanization. This is also an indication of the one-time extent of reliance on horse power. By 1948 they were said to be disappearing from the cornlands at a rate of 100,000 a year. More than 18,000 tons of horse meat was being shipped to Europe in cans, besides tonnages of pickled meat. Not surprising then that Harry Salter, President of Alberta Horse Breeders' Association, should voice fears of coming shortage and the view that with only five horses to a farm they should be very close to the minimum.

Happily, as it turned out, the worst fears were never realized. Much is owed to men like T. P. Devlin, who in the late '40s was honoured for 30 years' service as secretary to the breed association. His background was the great railway system that developed over Canada. And there was William M'Kirdy, Manitoba, who gave so much to Clydesdales and was made a life member of the association. His family established Mount Pleasant Farm – amongst imports was Woodend Gartly which bred them magnificent stock. There was David Binnie who went out there in 1910 to manage for R. H. Bryce Farms at St Charles, and after 14 years began on his own with Clydes based on Doune Lodge stock. Three years later his barn burnt down and he lost them but went on doggedly and bred some Grand Champions.

These were the sort of men who kept the flag flying, so that the 1952 Toronto Fair could still muster 140 Clydesdales even with mechanization complete, and when members of the Clydesdale Horse Association of Canada meet at that event for their AGM they are still at least 70 strong, with some 560 transactions to report, although these days no more than a dozen may be imports. In 1978 John Young from the home country attended the Fair and made history anew with the first Canadian-bred stallion, by Canadian sire and dam, being bought for export back to the UK. The breeder was Wreford Hewson, of Ontario. The grandsire of that horse, Belmont Ideal (30499), was five times Grand Champion at Toronto, and the only horse to equal that was J. E. Faulkner's famous Lochinvar (21417) that won 15 such awards throughout Canada and the United States.

In Australia it was not until gold was discovered in the 1850s that draught horse breeding, principally in Victoria, received any real boost. The originals were chiefly old New South Wales stock crossed with Cleveland, Old English dray horses, and then Suffolks with some Clydesdales. The last made their mark for active and weighty stock, although a report in 1870 suggested that in ten years only 30 stallions –

mostly Clydes – had been imported. But breeders were prepared to pay handsomely, as for example when H. Gordon Glassford of Jippsland paid 935gns for the imported stallion Big Gun. Two of the earliest to go out were Blackleg (71) bred by S. Clark in Campbeltown in 1856, and Blacklock (72) a year later, from R. Anderson of Wigtownshire.

Some good sales were reported from Tasmania. One farmer wrote: 'Had we 50 Clyde mares for every Clyde horse our plough and road teams would soon be better worth looking at . . . we are plainly destined to have not a vestige of any other breed left here soon.'

The move to publish a Clydesdale Stud Book in Australia did not come about until September 1914, and a breed society was set up in Victoria a year previously. There was also an Australian stud book for draught horses which entered both Clydesdales and Shires. Rivalry seems, however, to have been played down, even if there was pleasure in Edwin Roberts of Essendon taking the overall championship at Melbourne Royal in 1913 with the Clyde stallion Captain Dale (15764), Harviestoun bred. That was probably a much-needed boost too, because up to then the fashionable Clydesdale had been dubbed by the down-to-earth Aussies as 'a mere caricature' of a draught horse. And later, when with the War the draught horse trade there slumped, the downturn was attributed to a 'revulsion' against shadowy or weaker types of horses then available.

Things took a turn for the better in the early '20s and coincidentally it was Harviestoun influence again that achieved it. W. Moore Black of Corring, Victoria, bought Kerr's Flashdale (20576) by Dunure Footprint, when the Northern Stud was dispersed. The stallion cost 1,570gns, but it was a good investment and did the trick for Australian draught horse improvement. The stallion was kept from shipment in 1923 to take the Cawdor Cup under his new owner's name – the first and probably last Australian to win. An interesting point about the stallion is that the dam was a Baron's Pride and the line went back to Old Times (597) with mares that bore the eel stripe characteristic of the Highland Pony. So the Rosey family line doubtless went back to strong native stock, improved by the prepotent Baron's Price blood. Harviestoun knew pedigrees and what could be achieved.

Moore Black bought another Cawdor Cup winner in 1928 with A. Murdoch's Orange Blossom and he also had J. P. Sleigh's Wells Mescal. Such bold purchases led to triumph at Sydney Royal in 1925 when he won male and female championships, his supreme being Drumcross Radiant (18323) then 13 years and weighing over a ton. Then in 1927 he held a stud sale and Flashdale made top of 2,050gns to C. S. Rodda of Warracknabeal – the horse was deliberately poisoned a year later. Rodda had also bought Mescal at 1,850gns and other top horses.

Falkiner and Sons had the largest pedigree stud in Australia at that time, and a sale which they held realized £143 average for 78 head. Captain A. E. T. Payne of Yarraview had another good lot and his return was £179 average. This was one of the earliest Clydesdale strongholds in Victoria and the owner presented the equivalent of a Cawdor Cup for competition at the Royal Agricultural Society there.

This seems to have been a period of revival in heavy horse breeding throughout Australia. A Clydesdale Society was formed in Queensland in 1926 and two years later the Royal Show had entries of 208 – a rise of 76 in a year. A. Gillis of Newmarket, Victoria, had the champion in Rising Morn (20639) and Wells Mescal won for mares.

It seems paradoxical that the depression of the '30s saw the upsurge in horses continuing, so much so that the National Horse Association noted a return to horse labour with prices trebled. This was the time when two Scotsmen undertook some notable export deals. One was Hugh McGregor of Hazeldene, Kaniva, Victoria, who had been a stallionman in his native Stirling; the other was David Adams, who in 1934 if not earlier took in four stallions and six fillies to average £416 apiece. It must have been one of these, a filly by All's Well, which Adams sold to Glenn Brothers of Tilden for 295gns. She was reserve at Melbourne Royal the following year, and he promptly bought her back for return to Scotland.

Adams was in overall charge in 1936 of what must have been the largest Clydesdale shipment ever to Australia and New Zealand, with two boats out from Liverpool with 40 head on board. The feeding stuffs were almost a cargo in themselves – it was always essential to keep the stock in good condition throughout so that they took the eye of purchasers waiting on the quayside for their arrival. Included in this batch was the Cawdor winner Rosetta, which subsequently made 1,500gns in New Zealand; and the stallion Strathore Streamline that made 1,700gns.

At the first Australian foal show held at Nhill, Victoria, in that year, the winner was W. G. Wilkinson's Rosemeath Benefit and McGregor had the male ticket with Munificent (22379) with two of his Hazeldene mares female and reserve at Melbourne Royal and elsewhere. They were fine advertisements for this shipper. Listening to him recall those early years as exporter conveyed something of the pioneering that was done for the breed – not to mention the stockmanship skills and business expertise involved. Rewards were good for the few who could buy and ship successfully and bear the risks. Altogether he took out about 70 head, and every one landed alive and usually in show form. An advantage was that he could always rely on beating the New Zealand exporters: their imports needed time to recover from sea sickness whereas the trip to Australia was mostly in fine weather after Ceylon (Sri Lanka), and the rolling of the boat exercised the horses' muscles and joints to keep them fit. He saw to it that they were all innoculated against colds and this proved effective too. The season started at Perth, Western Australia, and finished at Adelaide where there was a strong Clydesdale settlement in the York peninsula.

McGregor, who had emigrated originally because the family farm was not large enough to offer prospects, spent several years as a stud manager on Wymburgh. He recalled the first combine harvester, developed from a stripper invented by Hugh Mackay who had a blacksmith's shop in the bush. One man would drive 8–10 horses yoked to this machine, sometimes abreast or in tandem, and he maintained they were as easily handled as a pair. A team driver was paid £2 a week plus board and £4 during harvest. When he first went out horse prospects must have looked poor, because the move to tractors was just starting. There were so many horses up for sale that no-one bought and they were simply being chased off farms and into the bush. That went on for five years, when wheat suddenly fell from 5s or $1.30 to 1s 10d or 30–50 cents a bushel and could not economically be grown by tractor and bought fuel – which explains why in 1935 Clydesdales were making up to 300gns at Sydney Royal.

When arriving with a boatload McGregor used to telegraph the prospective purchasers ahead. Then there would be a dockside parade, often with great enthusiasm and spirited bidding for the choicest lots. One of his earliest aboard 'SS Taranaki' included a filly, Hazeldene Merrymaid by Dupplin Castle, said to have been one of the dearest to go into Western Australia. Another time he sold a stallion, Bandolier, to the Galloway Stud – interestingly enough the next generation of that family took back several prize-winners themselves during a visit in 1963 including Brown Brothers' champion Glororum Prince. At that time they still ran a stud of 40 horses and were supplying geldings to Melbourne.

Both McGregor and Adams were several times honoured by presentations from home breeders, as recognition of their promotional work. Adams took over some 150 horses in the years 1923–39, which must have represented a tidy cash outlay.

The decline of the draught horse hit Australia in 1945–48 with many good animals ending up as dog meat. There was a notably doleful report from Adelaide saleyards of three-year-old Clydes selling for 35s each. As elsewhere in the world they were to stage the great comeback.

At Hamilton in New Zealand there is a Clydesdale Agricultural Museum, but that is simply keeping a complete record of agricultural development. The horses, whilst figuring prominently in past history, are still very much valued in the present; indeed Clydesdales are the only draught breed. The earliest importations are believed to have been three mares and a stallion to Otago in 1860, with the first owners W. H. Valpy of Forbury, and John Nimmo of W. Taieri. These were supplemented by later imports and in trading with Australian breeders.

James Kilpatrick was impressed with New Zealand's Clydesdales and stated that the best he had seen in Australia was Great Count, bred in New Zealand. As far back as the early 1900s he had offered £1,000 for Baron Bold, said to have been the finest ever foaled south of the line and he was on Patrick's Popetunoa Stud which dispersed in 1912 with £128 average.

The breed society was formed in New Zealand in 1911, publishing a stud book three years later. They were fortunate in having James Rankin, one of McNeilage's assistants with the parent body as the first secretary. He resigned in 1918 and from 1927–66 they had Robert McCay from Ulster, who was followed by S. N. Barnes.

In the '30s A. M'Nicol's Clevedon stock was much in evidence, especially through the stallion Gold Glint (20845) bred at Warrix. He won Auckland's championship three years in succession.

Currently enthusiasts in New Zealand are as keen as anywhere in the world, and whilst high costs of shipment may deter, they now have the stock to keep quality high. Furthermore, interest in driving and field-work is popularizing heavy horses fast.

South Africa was quite a good market for Clydesdales, but not until the early part of this century as the practice was to rely on toughish ponies rather than heavy draught horses. It was in 1901 that the Government imported 150 Clydesdale mares for use by Cape Town Harbour Board. Most of these were supplied by the Montgomerys and seemingly they landed when in winter coat in the midst of the summer heat, which was not the best of starts. However they were later tried at an experimental farm in the Transvaal and proved extremely useful, but work such as ploughing and transport was still being done by oxen up to 1907. When they were ultimately replaced, the Clydesdales helped the transition.

The Argentine was an active market, with exports dating back to before 1880. They must have been plentiful too, and the Argentinians certainly bought good stock – a stallion named McFarlane was said to be one of the highest-priced imports. One of the most astounding showing incidents ever occurred at the Palermo Show in the 1920s, for by error a Clydesdale class was paraded before Shire judges. When this was discovered the parade was repeated before the right breed experts, and the leading horses were put down to fourth place. It satisfied all concerned as proof that there were indeed differences in outlook and type between the two breeds.

Russia was another useful outlet for stock, with a shipment of 33 Clydesdales going there before the turn of the century – to Professor Kuleschoff for experimental breeding. In 1904 Montgomerys sent 16 – mostly Baron's Pride, the bloodline the whole world wanted. Instrumental in fostering the early trade was R. W. Eddison of Fowlers Engine Works, Leeds.

Continental traffic in Clydesdales was always a feature, despite the prominence of Belgian and Percheron breeds. It was the greater moving capacity which attracted buyers. There was an active breed society in Germany and shows were well supported. At one time they branded all the horses with a bold 'C' under a symbolic crown – this to confirm registration and to protect against fraudulent claims.

Ireland was another active breeding area and between 1846 and 1871 there were 206 sires entered, which was about twice the Suffolk strength. They were close enough to home territory to be able to lease good premium stallions, a practice which has continued with deputations frequently in attendance at leading shows. Although the fact is never mentioned there seems little doubt that the Clydesdale played its part in the development of the Irish draught horse which is now so much hailed as a breed. This is not least for the role it plays in the production of outstanding light horses – show jumpers and eventers plus the ubiquitous Irish hunter of international renown.

The Clydesdale certainly made its mark in the world, proved a grand ambassador and great pioneer of new farming techniques. Today the role may be somewhat different but wherever enthusiasts of the heavy horse gather will be found an undiminished reverence and appreciation of this breed. It has grown in stature with the realization of its achievements in those days before tractors and when the Prairies were but barren lands.

Nine

The World's Work Horse

One New Year's day, the poet Robert Burns wrote a salutation to his old mare Maggie. She was a Clydesdale beyond all doubt and he was expressing the affection and admiration which all farmers then and now feel for their working partners. In harness they were the companions of endless arduous and lonely hours' toil. None knew better than the men handling the lines or reins just what exertions and elements they suffered together; or the full extent of their capabilities without tiring or stumbling. Character counted as well as capacity, and these horses had good natures which commanded love in return.

Even with two tons behind them the Clydesdales were smart movers – they could walk four miles an hour, and some would say trot seven or eight. We tend, naturally enough, to picture them in rural setting behind plough or harvester, but in truth the majority were hauling away in city streets. Hundreds would be kept by hauliers such as Pickfords, the railway companies, or co-ops, and they drew every sort of cart, tramways, canal barges and – yes – even the equivalent of the tread-mill. Wherever there was need of energy or power these heavy horses supplied it.

Burns' old mare was 25 years old and had bred a succession of replacements – a fact acknowledged in his tribute to her. Lord Rowallan in the '20s had a gelding of 37 years and mare of 35 years that had worked together as a pair on the same farm for 32 years. This was an exceptional team perhaps, but there were many of 20 years upwards doing the same and keeping fit and sound for daily work.

That familiar slogan 'Keep the lorry in view' had sense to it, because pulling power was what these horses needed above all else. Breeders for commercial use never forgot this – men like John Smith of Broompark, who must have had great satisfaction from selling good weighty geldings to city galvanizing works and timber merchants, where they would be pulling from two to four tons a day.

In the States they valued this power so highly that they held pulling contests. On one occasion a dynamometer test in Iowa saw two horses weighing 1,400lb each making a tractive pull of 2,050lb. A Canadian-bred team of Belgian horses averaging 1,850lb once did a 3,100lb pull, which serves to illustrate that weight was linked with performance.

Horses lived off the farm and could be cheaply kept, and this was an important feature of their economy as compared to the later tractors. An estimated £5–£6 a week possibly covered the dozen horses needed on a 400-acres farm with only a portion of it arable land. When eventually three tractors replaced them it was estimated the cost was 12s a day each to operate. Allowance must be made for bias but hauliers' costings provide more detail. In the mid-'20s, for example, Aberdeen Cleansing Department kept 60 Clydesdales which averaged eleven years of service, cost 15s 5d a week to feed and bed, and 2½d for veterinary care, and which ate 15lb hay, 12lb oats and 3lb bran apiece.

A costing from another city enterprise, covering a stock of 140 horses quotes: '8 hour day, 313 days p.a. average cost horse-drawn of 3s 7d against 5s 1⅓d electric vehicles. Drivers wages 1s 2¼d hr + 2½d per day insurance. Feed 2s 11½d, preparation 5½d, saddlery, depreciation, shoeing, stabling and repairs taken into account.'

What proved the undoing of the cart horse was the reluctance of men to work at weekends, and to care for their charges at the beginning and end of the day in necessary and demanding stable routines.

Officially the last recorded use of horse teams pulling corn binders was at Abbeytown, Cumbria, in 1962. In fact, though, some farms never stopped using horse-power and surprisingly large units have continued full cultivation with as many as five pairs of horses.

Major industry developed in the provision of agricultural and other equipment for harnessing horse power. This has been lost sight of but it should not be under-valued since the transition from oxen to heavy-horse-power was of major importance. Such tackle as corn threshers were quite sophisticated and geared to horse power, the animal being walked patiently round and round on special lanes around the main drive-shaft on a treadmill principle. There were many similar applications.

Proper and devoted care was a big factor in keeping horses fit for work and Clydesdale men were the world's best. They were dedicated and generous with their charges, with the significant result that their farming required less horse power. If this seems beyond belief there are statistics on record showing that an average of 3.9 horses per 100 acres was needed against a general average of 4.2, based on average or medium land under four or five course rotation. The probability is that this owed much to improved strains as compared with very ordinary stock.

Spring work was the testing time, when the horses' hair was often dried out and condition lost during the winter. They would be ill-prepared for a sudden hard onrush of seasonal work, if conditions allowed them on the ground earlier than usual. A favourite remedy would be plenty of boiled barley, with a few swedes mixed in when they came in from work, and an extra heavy supper of corn in late evening. Incidentally, disputes between master and men on the subject of corn rations occurred regularly. Many liked to overdo their charges with six bushels of corn a week for a pair, whilst four, plus roots and fodder was recommended if in work.

Feeding a Clydesdale stallion out on its district, covering perhaps 80 mares a season and walking up to ten miles a day, could be quite tricky. They invariably got plenty of corn, 14lb of good hay, 3–4lb white peas (beans caused itchy legs) and 1lb bruised linseed cake two or three times a week. On Saturday there was the ritual of the bran mash and a light weekend.

As long ago as 1885 Jacob Wilson told The Farmers' Club that over-feeding was the cause of many highly bred horses being lost. He thought it was especially bad for show mares which never bore a foal afterwards. He was a man who had given 400gns for the hire of a Clydesdale stallion for one season with good results and so knew something about it. There is no doubt that stock for sale was overdone. If put to harness too soon afterwards the horses would founder.

That horses were often overtaxed in work is well known, and there have been many reports from earlier days of them being asked to haul up to eight tons in a day until they dropped. For a time sales by weight were popular, particularly in America, and these at least had the merit of illustrating how easily it could be lost. One estimate showed that ¼cwt could go in the course of a five-mile walk. So it was not without reason that grooms went to great lengths to see their charges got generous treatment.

Doubtless the various Horsemens' Societies, which flourished in some rural areas, had views on feeding methods. They also had secret 'Words' and rituals which made them almost a freemasonry of Clydesdale lore. One password of entry to the secret society asked the question: 'Where did you last leave your plough?' and the strange answer would be 'Beneath the moon, behind a stance at the end of a well ploughed rig.' They had their secret potions for fertility and condition too – some of them dangerous as they involved the use of arsenics or acids with severe irritant effects. In 1932 there was a case in Durham of a groom being given a wrong prescription by a chemist, resulting in a Clydesdale stallion being burned by carbolic acid instead of having a dose of carbolic oil. It was risky business.

From a veterinary point of view Clydesdales were easier to keep fit than most breeds, although extremes in conformation could bring problems. Andrew Montgomery used to say that the horse past 17 hands high was all the worse for it, whilst William Brown, a prominent vet. in the '20s, complained that breeders would cite the 'No foot, no horse' rule but had adhered to it so long that they forgot the rest and finished up with no carcase.

It follows that when certain lines of breeding had major influence there was always risk of troubles spreading. There was, for instance, a major furore in 1900 in America over suspected stringhalt cases with a very good stallion and his son slaughtered as risks – uselessly as it turned out.

The big problem of earlier years however, especially about 1913, was equine viral arteritis – known as 'Pink-eye' – which damaged the arteries. Many valuable stallions were lost in a major outbreak, whilst other stock might survive but be of no further use. There were reports of owners and grooms 'forcing pints of whisky, beer or port down patients' throats' in attempts at cures. Rest and warmth was felt to be more effective. Worse still in the Clydesdales' own country was Grass Sickness, responsible for the loss of many good horses with tragic wasting symptoms. Only in recent times has it been linked with midges, but there is still no antidote other than housing when conditions favour such pests.

What we can hardly appreciate now is that the huge populations of equines were so much at risk to any spread of infection. Losses could be nearly disastrous, and especially in young stock through the bacterial joint-ill at foaling and similar maladies. This is why the expertise of older grooms was so highly valued, even if their remedies seem laughable by contemporary standards.

Another factor which may be overlooked is that there was no sophistication in matters such as shoeing. Even horse clippers were at a premium and seemingly many grooms just resorted to the singeing lamp; happily no awful consequences resulted. As far as shoes are concerned we have tried plastics out, somewhat unsuccessfully, in recent times, but they were just as inventive a century ago. Innovations such as spring shoes or those without nails met with ready response, even although they were usually found wanting.

Heavy horse management certainly lacked scientific exactness, which the scale of use and need really required, but any shortcomings seem to have been amply compensated by the degree of skill and care horses received. Indeed it is doubtful if any class of stock, or certainly many of the people at the time, were ever as well tended as the Clydesdales of old. And the tradition is still upheld because there has never been scope for half measures; nor ever will be.

Ten

Harness and Wagons

Old farm carts and odd pieces of harness are nowadays counted as prized possessions, where a previous generation utterly discarded them. It is distinctly heartening too, that these things are not just sought as rarities for collection – they are wanted for active use with heavy horses. The shortage is such in fact that there is a return to cottage industry in making reproductions, using modern materials for economy and to save weight. This applies to farm implements as well and few would have dared prophesy that the horse-drawn models would return to production, after they had been cheerfully relegated to museums or converted to tractor use. But there is now a re-awakening interest in the possibilities of live horse power put for the first time to modern versions of plough, seed drill or mower, and of course using plastics and all the other developments of recent times which would make them very much less cumbersome and cheaper.

For very understandable reasons the history of heavy horse tackle has never really been researched, and yet it is a fascinating subject rich in regional variations and patterns. To begin with one must distinguish between working gear and show sets of harness, because the latter are much more decorative with fancy touches which owe little to utility, and indeed can totally obscure the lines of a good horse. For work use the heavy set is plain and practical, with still the hint of local designs and styles which become very much accentuated for display purposes. Even within a district however, one must allow for variation, simply because fashion dictated. Possibly rival saddlers in a market town might be spurred into demonstrations of their craft which horsemen were always keen to encourage as they in turn also sought to impress.

The principle item has always been the bridle, almost universally blinkered or blindered with flaps on either side of the eyes to prevent other than forward vision and with bit attached; and from the rings a

short rein, used only as a bearing rein looped over the hame to keep the
head up. This rein would not always be used, depending on whether the
animal might be head-strong or a stumbler, and for control long reins
would be buckled to the bit rings. Clydesdale whips were always unique
in preferring to use lines of rope for driving, in preference to leather
reins which were the more universal choice. Lines have always been
chosen with plough teams, because they offer flexibility and grip better
beneath the hand on the stilts or handles of the plough. Possibly in the
wetter northern climes it was found that leathers proved slippery,
though I prefer them myself. Even in show turnout the Clydesdales
would be in lines, although with the best set in use, very proudly
whitened. Another distinct feature has always been the looping of these
lines from the bit to beneath the shaft and up to the whip's hands;
whereas the majority of breeds are driven from reins passing overhead
through collar rings. This different line of control could produce an
improved action, but whether it was adopted consciously or not is
another matter.

Horse collars are objects of great fascination, not least because it is
not obvious how they may be fitted. This applies especially to Clydesdales since for work or show the collars have extreme points. One would
think that there was no advantage in this highly stylized version and it
is attributed to a fashion which has endured. The universal type of collar
has a low-set neatly rounded point to it; in some arable areas using
Suffolks with broad necks they often had squared-off tops which were
quite decorative. With the collar, fitting into a wooden slot all around
the front, go the hames or metal points which carry the tugs or hooks
for chains acting as the pulling connection to cart or implement. Again
Clydesdale hames go high and curve outwards at the top like antennae.
Hames are usually permanently affixed to the collar and the whole
apparatus is slipped over the horse's head by turning it upside down,
slipping it over, then adjusting it correctly. A good fit is essential, for
this, after all, is the power drive. The heavy pad or saddle carries the
body girth and the bridge or channel running over the centre holds a
flat close-linked chain, which connects at either end to hooks on the
shafts. In the gear for plough or team work a simple flat pad strap to
carry the draught chains may suffice. Attached to the back of the saddle
is the complex arrangement of leather straps known as the breechings,
with a crupper that goes around the tail to hold the saddle in place and
a lower breech band around the lower thighs which has a braking effect
and in backing a horse leans into the breech. This breeching set is not
used in team work.

A set of cart harness is solid and heavy, but then it has to stand considerable strain. There may be variations, according to use and personal

choice. Some, particularly in the States, employ leather traces instead of chains; or a breast-collar for light draught. But basically the yoke is fairly standard and this is a good thing.

The difference between show and working turnout is mainly in the trimmings, but finer leather and even patent leather can be used. Decorations include numerous horse brasses on the breastplate linking collar to girth, with a brass facepiece on fancy browband and mono-grammed blinkers. Hames may be chromed and have special tips to them – Clydesdale men like thistle tops and collar edges are sometimes trimmed with tiny tassels or coloured woollen loops, as also are the breechings and other parts of the harness. Saddles invariably carry intricate arches or ornaments such as plumes or bells. Floral harness decorations have long been an art associated with Clydesdales and some rare craftsmanship has come out of cottages where the occupants spent many a long winter night making intricate designs from ribbons and now plastic. Decorated harness classes at shows are a speciality and particularly associated with this breed.

Traditional English farm wagons for heavy horse haulage have been a feature since the early nineteenth century, but curiously enough not so much associated with Clydesdales. Clydesdales have mostly been put to what are called 'farm carts', or tumbrils as infamously used in the French Revolution. These sturdy-built two-wheelers are really box carts but have often been called 'Scotch' carts, as they were first built in Scotland and sold in considerable numbers all over Britain. They were, and are still, used for hauling manure, root crops and other goods and would hold up to two tons, which was as much as a horse could draw. They would tip and had giant wheels of considerable weight when iron-shod. Modern adaptations of the design move freely on rubber tyres.

The most common vehicle seen now, particularly at shows, is the four-wheeled lorry, well sprung and with turning front axle. These at one time had very wide use for all haulage work and were a standard design but appearing in all manners of liveries and hand-painted decoration. They could have a single horse between shafts, or a pair, and teams still use them. Sometimes side boards are fitted and show versions often have headboards and high seat for the whip. Being universal, the lorry was known as a 'rully' in the northern counties of England, sometimes as a 'trolley', and descriptively as a 'flat' elsewhere.

Harnessing up to such vehicles is much simpler than may appear. The shafts are laid down and the horse backed in between them, stepping carefully to avoid breakage. Such is the temperament of the heavy horse, and Clydesdale in particular, that it will stand steady whilst the carter or whip lifts the shafts, throws the saddle chain over and carefully moves around the other side to latch it and hold the shafts steady. Then the draught chains are linked from collar hame hook to vehicle, the lines or reins put through and away you go.

When teams are involved the gear is simple, but the network of chains and belts confusing. One of today's leading exponents with Clydesdales is Hugh Ramsay of Millisle, Wigton, and his demonstration six-horse team has delighted crowds all over the country. He has been almost the only whip to bring such an equipage out onto the show circuit, following the American versions which have regularly been a great spectacle. Ramsay has driven eight horses but admitted to me that so many reins were a bit of a handful, and in arenas with limited space six at a trot is about right. The biggest hitch on record was probably that of Richard Sparrow in Iowa, who reputedly had 40 horses yoked and some mileage of rein.

It is of course a major outlay to put a six-horse team together nowadays, even if it is possible to get them matched. Ramsay reckons a good gelding at about £2,000; then there is special show harness which is almost beyond price – his is kept in a specially heated tack room – plus lorry and travelling expenses. Then there is the feed – perhaps 12lb oats each a day and good hay. In his case the horses are put to work about the farm, live off the produce of it, and are frequently traded. Moreover the publicity value of such an outfit must attract sponsorship, as well as the film work which has become almost a regular feature.

Brewery companies have traditionally shown the Shire and Suffolk heavy horses, whilst Clydesdales have had their flag flown handsomely for years by the Scotch whisky distillers, James Buchanan and Company, whose show turnouts earn praise, and warm affection too for the drays which even yet work on city streets. A winner and favourite is their gelding Chester, who stands an unbelievable 19.2 hands high and is rated one of the biggest horses in the country. Whether pure Clyde or not is anyone's guess, but when he had to rest in a sling to ease a leg trouble on one occasion, their chief carter Robert Woods slept in his box every night for a month to ensure he was all right. That is the sort of dedication Clydesdales command. Mr McIntosh, manager, is convinced there is nothing to beat their horses on short haul work and is even finding young carters keen to work in stables, though admittedly the 7.30 am to 4 pm routine is easier than in the old days.

Stable routines vary and Mr Ramsay quotes a common pattern on farms with working horses:

6 am feed, clean-out and set fair
Then breakfast
7.30 to 12 noon ploughing or other work
One hour break and nosebag or short bite
1 pm to 5 pm back at work

6 pm After grooming and stables, main feed
(Feeds: one-third bran two-thirds bruised oats and good hay)

Anyone familiar with traditional folk songs, known as bothy or stable ballads, will be aware that daily routines resulted in a rich heritage being handed down. In the days of large stables the horsemen were numerous and stables were happy places, reflecting a contented if hard way of life. They sang as they curry combed or brushed these great horses and they loved their work and charges. It is immensely satisfying that some part of such folklore lingers on – indeed that we should be rediscovering the source of their satisfaction.

Eleven

Their War Effort

Lest we forget. The present generation realizes nothing of the historic role the heavy horse, and Clydesdales in particular, played in warfare. This chapter is in the nature of a tribute and reminder of our indebtedness. The horses' function was very well described by Lord Rosebery, speaking in the House of Lords as far back as 1873, when he declared: 'The horse is the adjunct of commerce, the implement of agriculture, and the engine of war.' Memorable words and in fact they were spoken in a period of acute shortage of horse-power which was the result of sacrifice in war. Thousands of work horses were being imported, and seen to be notably inferior to our breed in courage, endurance and stamina.

Only the men who shared the mud and the hell of war fully appreciated the role of the draught horses, and it is doubtful if they were ever given adequate recognition in official circles. After World War I however, the soldiers who had worked with them were loud in praise and very proud of their gallant Clydesdales. Moreover they saw to it that they were brought down the lines to rest as regularly as the troops themselves. They must have needed respite, too, from the toil of hauling artillery out of entrenched positions, not to mention removal from the noise and carnage all around them.

Major-General Sir John Moore of the Army Veterinary Service gave the short-legged, sturdily built types of Clydesdales a good record in war, even in the forward areas. At the same time he dared to criticize variable type and qualities found in horses taken to France. Hardly surprising one might think, considering the way they were impressed for service by agents searching them out far and wide from reluctant owners who needed them so badly for food production at home.

The Australian Veterinary Corps apparently found Clydesdales best for military work in the heavy conditions that prevailed, whilst for artillery purposes they especially liked the produce of the Thoroughbred stallion from the Clydesdale mare. The Canadian Corps were similarly minded, liking short-legged and round barrelled types the best. That T.B. cross to Clydes, particularly using the smaller sorts of mares, was especially popular for the production of carriage horses, and even earlier than 1911 their endurance had been tested in artillery warfare with Hackney crosses as a good alternative.

That the war used up huge stocks of equines can be judged from one estimate in 1910 that 170,000 were needed to put the army on a war basis. And that was long before losses were incurred. It was also only the home country's contribution. There were even reports that dummy horses on rockers were being ordered as a means of confusing the enemy!

As a part of the war effort the breeding of Clydesdales was stepped-up and voluntarily those that could be spared from home use were sent out to France, as well as plans laid to offer good examples of the breed for replenishing stocks in countries devastated by the conflict. The Clydesdales' docility was a characteristic that was valued, particularly when they were put into the hands of men unused to dealing with draught horses. Belgian and Percheron crossbreds were often liable to be kickers in the army lines, causing casualties amongst the men, whereas the Clydes retained an equable temperament. Other useful factors were an ability to manage and keep condition on limited forage allowances, pulling the load nevertheless and weathering the wet and cold too.

Many amusing stories were told of attempts to deceive agents seeking Clydesdales for the army. One farmer instructed his son that whilst he was absent at market if agents called he was to say that one particularly likely gelding was vicious and unsound. The army duly came, heard the tale . . . and just paid rather less for the horse because of his reported faults.

Towards the end of the Great War there was report of a particularly big push in France and Clydesdales were pulling 60-pounder guns, supply wagons and horse ambulance lorries under terrible front-line conditions with roads under shellfire and carts down to the axles in mud. A serving soldier wrote home at the time in these terms: 'The horses' high spirits and tameness won through and many times they had to help other slugs out of the rut'. Another reported that all breeds were losing flesh along the Hindenburg lines but that the Clydes were always looking cheery. Sad that when demobilized in 1918–19 in their thousands the weary and out of condition veterans simply glutted the market and went to the slaughterers in droves . . .

That war finished a historic role for heavy horses, beginning in their days as chargers; never again were they needed in battle lines. But

World War II nevertheless saw them in the front of a massive ploughing-up campaign in the fight for food supplies. The tractor was still making its way into service and with 40 per cent more land under plough horse power was necessary . . . and the land girls loved them.

Wartime rations for work horses were 9lb grain a day with up to 6½lb extra if on continuous work and appeal to the feeding stuffs controller was successful. When 3cwt a month was the ration for stallions at stud it resulted in such strong protest that a 1cwt supplement was given. On balance one suspects that with less corn they were fitter and comparison of fertility and foaling averages would have been interesting.

The only casualties in the last war seem to have been those travelling to the States in ships which were torpedoed. In one notable loss a stud of eleven horses destined for August A. Busch of St Louis, was entirely wiped out.

Whether in the front line or in a country in state of siege the heavy horse has served. It is extraordinary that in all these ways it has such common bond with man.

Twelve

Hobby Horses

Studying heavy horses of all kinds, and Clydesdales in particular, has become a fascinating hobby and interest for countless people. The indications are that such enthusiasts will be increasingly catered for in the future with the establishment of special centres where they can learn to drive a team, study horses and tackle, and see everything actually at work: the scope is enormous.

As a youth I was initiated into stable practice, even though dwarfed by the towering giants munching their hay so placidly above me. The magic atmosphere of stables has to be experienced and is never forgotten, with the all-pervading and almost sickly sweetness of best-cured hay and fresh straw bedding, combining well with the quite acceptable smell of horses and the special richness of leather hide. These things permeate the senses, especially when allied to the sense of power associated with big animals, striking sparks with iron-shod and massive hoofs struck against unyielding cobble-stones.

There is, too, an orderliness about stables which is seldom found on farms or factories. Everything has its place and is somehow never out of it unless in use. Heavy horse tack is either on its rack, being cleaned, or on the horse's back. It is never cast idly aside in a corner. Similarly one does not ever (or so it seems) pick up a bridle and discover the bit-piece covered in newly-champed hay pieces. When taken off in front of stables it is automatic procedure to dunk it in the rainwater tub standing beside the door. Haphazard and unorthodox maybe, but simple good sense affects all things to do with the heavy horses.

The other impression which must assail the senses is that of peace and a leisurely attitude to work; which is anathema to some, but wonderfully soothing to others. You don't hasten with horses – you adopt the plodding gait, getting there all the faster too if the truth be told. It is rather curious that this should be so in animals manifestly capable of a galloping pace. They have adjusted, one suspects over centuries, to the pace of work and it is even possible that mankind can observe them closely to advantage in this regard. Clydesdales, after all, are the briskest movers in the heavy horse hemisphere, but it would be deceptive to suppose that they go everywhere at the trot: they make haste slowly, so to speak.

The only time one sees the heavies letting their pace go is when they are first released from work into the field for grazing and relaxation, especially after a lengthy period in stables; in springtime for example, after a winter indoors and a hard spell at the plough, then sudden release onto the freedom of springy turf without harness or impediment. Why, then you'll see the hairy fetlocks fly and the manes sweep out carelessly in the breeze, and there'll quite possibly be an unaccustomed buck or two for the sheer joy of it. Otherwise your heavy horse simply plods. Only a youngster green and senseless ever starts and offers the threat to bolt off. And he seldom does so, because the carter or whip senses any change instinctively and utters the timely cautionary and soothing word, with an imperceptible flick on the rein which reinforces it. Much of the language of the heavy horse world is unintelligible to fellow humans, beyond a restraining 'Whoa' or clicking 'Giddup up there,' and yet there is a constant communication – a dialogue they would call it nowadays – between man and horses, which is effective and companionable. It has to be said that crying out is not an essential ingredient to horse control.

Real control rests between the horse's mouth (the bit) and the whip's hands (via the rein or line) and the voice has habitually reinforced this link, simply because the hands may be engaged in steering the plough or other tasks and the 'feel' or contact is weak. Driving work horses cannot be compared to riding or driving the light horse, where communication is well defined and constant; necessarily so because it is a finely tuned animal accustomed to giving speedy responses. The slow-plodder has a more limited horizon, it knows the work routine, and answers to call or instinct or rein with auto-reflex action. It is quicker to stop than go; presumably because it pauses frequently and hastens rarely. A Clydesdale in the harvest field might just be clicked up to a trot drawing an unaccustomed empty wagon out over firm ground, but under load it finds its own willing pace and there's no more can be expected as the strain is taken on the collar and the great muscles bulge with effort.

This is not to imply that a whip or carter will have no influence – far from true. To see the combination working well together one must watch driving parades on the showgrounds, where it becomes clear that it is a skilled art. Untrammelled by loads or traffic considerations, the lines are taken in either hand and a close contact made with the bit, so that even the slightest inflexion of rein will be taken as a command. Pace is quickened by driving the horse up to the bit, which means urging it on without always releasing the rein, so that it becomes gathered into hand rather like a bent spring and as the hand gives it releases the spring or the energy and the animal becomes light and dances over the ground.

The Clydesdale's great attribute, as has been stated, is its stride, and this is quite exceptional. You can see it cover the ground in long strides which are graceful and light, evenly paced so that the hind hoof steps cleanly into the space flattened by the fore. This gives a good moving walk and at the trot covers quite a lot of ground, in comparison with others which may seem to be jinking along and in truth not getting anywhere much at all. Skilled driving will achieve this sort of pace and movement, although if the horse is not bred for it with the right conformation no wizard on the reins can do anything to correct it.

Now this aspect of the Clydesdale bears closer examination, because at shows in-hand (which means not driven or in harness) the judges spend endless time taking each entry in turn and having it walked and trotted back and forth under their keen eyes. They will stand directly behind or in front of the animal as it moves and I'll warrant that there will be a packed crowd right behind them scrutinizing every stride. The same, it must be said, is done with all other horses in-hand, including hunters, but there can be no mistaking the priority movement is given in the Clydesdale ring.

What watchers, including yourselves, must observe, is the action of the horse, striding boldly out right from the shoulder and really covering the ground – straight out. Looked at from behind you can see clearly through the legs, with no suggestion of hocks being bent or legs weaving in and out as they move. Keep the eyes on the legs because there is all the movement, curiously enough, and the upper part of the horse usually seems almost static, hanging back even as the handler runs alongside and ahead. This sight will reinforce the view that there is nothing fast about a heavy horse and it does not give any appearance of relishing speed as such.

One reason for this may well be a limited field of vision, which of course is not aided by the fact that the heavy horse spends most of its working life in blinkers. Probably more relevant is the limited way the heavy horse uses its back, as compared to the light horse. Watch a horse at the gallop and you are conscious that the back is arched and the legs gathered under to match. It is an athletic performance which is made possible by a streamlined conformation, which the Clydesdale or any other heavy horse simply does not have. 'Horses for courses' is an apt phrase.

Looking upwards into the bold eye of the horse you might incline to the view that it winks back with a depth of intelligence and wisdom undimmed through all ages. Is this so? I wish it were, but I frankly doubt it. There is no evidence of heavy horses being very bright, even if they don't tend to lose their marbles like some thoroughbreds. There used to be a circus which featured a performing Clydesdale in company with a Shetland pony, and it was an amusing act. But that is really the secret: the mind and the memory can be programmed quite effectively, and with docility bred in, the combination is useful within its limits.

In human stereotypes, the labourer may be slow and sure, dependable, but limited in his range of abilities, as compared with say the financier who is jet-set, calculating and nervous. So it is with equines and one should not look for performance outside the range of memory given to the heavy horse: within it there may be no equal. Don't forget too that there are differing levels of intelligence and the much shown and proud stud stallion is on a completely different stratum from the cart gelding.

Show-goers cannot fail to be impressed with the skilled way in which Clydesdales are turned out on parade, marvelling indeed at the fineness of silky hair on the fetlock, and the neatness of mane and tail plaiting. It is helpful to appreciate the relevance of all this to the display of conformation which is going on all around. That tail which is tucked up so neatly, for example, enables you and the judges to study the legs in action without hindrance; likewise the mane put up reveals the set of the shoulder and the way it moves. Hair in itself is an indication of condition and breeding; whether it is a fetish carried too far is an ongoing question.

It is hard work bringing any animal out for the show-ring, and in the case of a heavy horse can be extremely time-consuming and costly – but worth it because this represents the breeder or exhibitor's shop-window and interest is manifest. All down the years there have been arguments advanced against shows, but never any which provide satisfactory alternatives: for the simple answer is that there are none.

Not everyone has the fine experience of showing a horse, obviously, although all can share in the excitement and indeed glamour of the spectacle. The most attractive and colourful display, however, is in the harness classes. Most leading shows give facility for parades of the decorated horses, with awards for those with cleanest harness etc, as well as for parades of horses drawing carts or other vehicles. I hope the day will come when there will also be classes for those put to different implements and seen in various uses. It might well prove a stimulant to manufacturers who could turn their skills to devising tackle, especially for heavy horse power.

Larger national shows and leading county events are also now featuring competitions for blacksmiths and those who can shoe a horse. This again is a skilled art returning to favour and reflecting an aspect of rural industry for long closely allied to the use of heavy horses. It is useful to see how the farriers handle the task of shaping and paring these hoofs as big as dinner plates, then fit them with iron shoes which can be as individual as is needed. Shoes go back to 2000 BC, and although seemingly it is little changed in principle, in fact the art is such that conformation faults may be corrected and development directed without the aids appearing in any way obvious. Shoeing can be humane too, to prevent slipping or the horse striking into itself with tips of hind toes.

One way of displaying your own interest in heavy horses is to collect different types of horse-shoes – a very cheap and unusual hobby too, costing nothing at all. It is fascinating just how many rusty shoes can be found in town or country, as they are thrown away and rust but rarely disappear altogether. Nail them up, but be sure to put the toe downwards so the shoe holds the luck in!

Odds and ends of harness occupy many collectors' interests and in recent years it is amazing how values and collections have sprung up. One wonders why it took so long and so much of value was discarded, before it was realized just how fascinating this study could become. Bits in themselves offer infinite variety and many are very decorative when polished up, as also are the rings which accompany them. Bridles and other gear vary less but patterns across the regions show change.

Of course the major collectors' item is horse-brasses and these are a subject in themselves, with all too few people realizing that in different forms they are older than the horse – certainly harness or horse (possibly oxen) decorations have been traced back 2500 BC and it seems to have been a need for charms or deification which produced the early rich and varying designs.

Most horse brasses appear to have been a by-product of the Industrial Revolution, with many commemorative patterns, and some say that there are between 3,000 and 4,000 different patterns to be found. Certainly they are varied and usually localized; nowadays the reproductions are quite reasonable.

A collection of Clydesdale emblems would be of special significance and apart from horse brasses one could usefully seek out ornamental pieces. There is an endless field here in hames tips, blinker studs, saddle decorations and inscribed plates. This is history in subtle form and each item will have a story behind it.

Collecting implements would seem to have limitations for most people, but the surprising fact is that the interest has suddenly blossomed and knows no limits. The cottage garden will often have a horse-plough behind the flower bed and if you enquire the proud owner will tell you that hardly a week passes without someone stopping to plead for its sale. Many which have lain years rusting in the rig-end of the field have been dug out and lovingly restored. When completed there is nothing that shines brighter than the ploughshare and in traditional livery the plough was always brightly painted to the point of being garish.

There is no limit to the implement or mechanical range, but often Clydesdale fanciers will be content with a set of stretchers or chains. These were made of hardwood, polished and slightly curved, and tipped with bright metals in sets of three or more. They display masterly craftsmanship and are extremely decorative on a wall, especially when set with chains and other pieces. There is a wide range of similar tack.

Carts and wagons have, alas, become extremely scarce and dear, many uselessly but decoratively forming displays in hotel forecourts and similar places. They are at least preserved and available for all to climb upon and see. It would be of great value if rural craftsmen could be prevailed upon to reproduce more of the traditional designs to meet the need and enable more enthusiasts to drive or be driven behind a sturdy Clydesdale. Meantime we must appreciate the skills that even yet go into restoring the old stock, because many are emerging as good as new, lovingly remade and traditionally painted.

Following a hobby is the next best thing to being totally involved in the Clydesdale world, and it is heartening to know that the interest in these areas is greater than at any time before. And it means that the future is assured. Hobby interests are possibly a new and strange phenomenon to many farmers and they don't profess to understand them; which is strange because they are themselves the most enthusiastic collectors and patrons of nostalgia. I hope that increasingly many of them will be persuaded to share their knowledge and experience, and to give active encouragement to those who are keen but have less opportunity for participation.

Thirteen

Into the Future

With the Clydesdale breed striding very confidently into its new century, there is sudden realization that it is not in danger of being relegated to museum status even if still registered as a species in danger of becoming extinct. Thus there remains a question mark over the future *for* heavy horses rather than doubt any longer as to their actual survival. Those who have for long predicted the end of an era, and have been thoroughly pessimistic and gloomy, have been totally confounded – in fact they have lost heavily in selling up, missing out on the boom time that has returned. Fortunes were reversed so that the 100th report of the breed society could state with some confidence that demand for horses of the right type continued to be in excess of supply, and the state of the market generally extremely healthy. No sign there of defeatism, and an expanding membership and showing activity underlined the fact.

How strange it is that the unbelievable came to pass: that the one-time absurdly optimistic diehards who predicted the time would come again for heavy horses have been proved right. They believed it would be war which would re-establish their place – when in fact it was Arabs revaluing oil supplies and stirring thoughts of alternative sources of energy. When these included wind and wave power it was inevitable that horse-power in literal terms should be re-assessed too. There is scope for the Clydesdale in much the same way as we have already switched off our oil-heating and returned to using wood-burning stoves. This movement began with the Suez crisis in the '50s and has slowly gathered momentum ever since.

Not so long ago when I visited a 400-acre farm which was being worked entirely by the five pairs of horses, the owner was quite ada-mant that it was not done for sentiment but because he genuinely felt that they were economical and in the long run more reliable than mechanical power. The main snag was in securing the right tackle to complement them. Now there have been times when such claims would have been dismissed out of hand, if not mocked into the bargain, and it is interesting that this should no longer be the case and that increasingly the scientists and thinkers amongst us are inclined to stop and question. As the price and scarcity of finite energy forms are deliberated, so does the spotlight increasingly turn to the like of the draught horse.

There is little doubt that there are many jobs about the farm which a horse in harness can perform better than a machine, because it is amenable and knowing, can live off the land at low cost and besides can multiply rather than simply depreciate. Even in cities they are rediscovering the economy of the brewers' dray with a fine pair of horses as an economical form of delivery and a remarkably fine and effective advertising medium for the product too. There was a time when companies invested in show turn-outs simply for the promotional value (the National Coal Board was one) but increasingly they learn that it can do a useful job as well and may even displace the lorry.

This so-called 'renaissance' of the horse-powered farm has other attractions too. Increasingly and internationally there are strongly advanced views that this could be the correct concept on environmental grounds, with many communities on religious and ethnic lines insistent that horses have values in accord with their beliefs which reject oil-powered energy. Of course it would be poor judgement to take such argument to extremes. There will be no return of work horses to the prairie-lands, but smaller diversified farming units all over the world could use them, as also for logging work and any short haul tasks. I rather like the quote attributed to Buck Buckles, who works a 9,000-acres spread in Nebraska for the Shadbolt Cattle Company, and who drawled: 'I like to mess with a horse, because they do so damn much for you that a tractor won't . . . You can be pitching hay and tell 'em to "Gee" or "Haw" . . . you turn a tractor loose and try to pitch hay, you're a busy son of a gun and most of the time you're a-chasing that tractor.' More sound logic from this source added: 'You've gotta think like a horse, or you can't go along with him. If you don't think like a horse, it don't do no good to have one; else everything you do with him will be backwards, and you won't get nothing done.' That's real sense for you!

Buck Buckles has a point which is crucial to the future of the horse, and fundamental to the limits of expansion; namely the need for skilled labour capable of understanding how to work with them. Where are the people today who can think like a horse? That virtue was one bred in, as son followed father, and on reaching majority was given not only the secret 'Horseman's Word' but also the formula for a mystic polish for show harness and other lore besides.

A principal snag with any livestock, and horses are no exception, is that they require attention 365 days, and sometimes nights, in the year, which hardly approximates to the 35-hours week. It is also a far cry from a Labour Commission Inquiry of 1893 which was told that the men started in stables at 5 am to yoke at 7 am and finished at 6.30 pm in summer. On Sundays they had to appear in stables in the morning, but employers did not insist on them returning in the evening, and it was no longer the custom for them to be back for family prayers. In 1869 another government committee reported that things were even harder with the hours from 5 am to 7 pm and many boys began at seven years old and must often walk 10–12 miles daily over ploughed land. Wages for a full ploughman were £24 per annum, plus ten bowls of meal, potatoes planted, a cottage and garden, and total value was £38 per annum.

Times certainly have changed; and for the better in that regard. But stable routine has not altered and there are no short cuts, even if machine grooming is possible. So it must be seen as a calling and a labour of love. The need for job satisfaction has crept in again. Fortunately a new generation is beginning to evaluate things anew and sees profit in work which is freer from stress and truly satisfying. It is also work which liberated women can enjoy, where once they were almost banned from entering stables. But there is an urgent need for training to be given and there are signs that this is already being considered.

One major area of development is likely to be in heavy horse centres, already established in parts of England and in the States. Clydesdale enthusiasts have been slow to react to this trend and yet it is not going to be long delayed. These should not be seen, let me hastily point out, as museums for the collection and display of a dying species. Instead they are an alternative shop window to the show-ring, tourist attractions, and offer scope for visitors to do as well as see. They should be able to ride in a wagon and try their hand on the ribbons by driving a Clydesdale in harness. Let them help to muck out stables and watch all forms of work routines. And above all training courses should be held on organized lines. With subtle marketing of promotional packages in the form of liveried turnouts, this sort of centre could become very big business indeed. It deserves to be tried out.

There is another expression of a new wave of enthusiasm to be found in the shape of heavy horse work-ins, which have to an extent replaced the traditional and often very tedious ploughing matches. At these mammoth events all the old crafts are given scope for demonstration, and clearly everything to do with horse work in the fields is given opportunity. Thousands of people attend such events, coming

from far afield and successfully mingling town with country in the way
it has been hoped for over years of endeavour. It does seem as though
the leisure age has cast new thought on the erstwhile laborious times,
with environmental issues dominant, and above all a need to indulge in
nostalgia. Hence this is again the age of the craftsman and woman and
work-ins have nothing in common with trade union disputes in this
sense; rather is it the quiet sense of satisfaction in seeing a craft
revived, a wagon renovated, or a wheel shod. Even in the height of the
Clydesdale boom in former years there was never such widespread
interest or such sentiment and scope to be tapped.

When in 1980 the District Council in Aberdeen, the centre of offshore
oil business, voted to replace a motor van with a pair of Clydesdale
horses and a cart, it made headlines the world over. Patiently it was
explained to an astounded Press that the horses and tackle cost £6,800
compared with £8,500 for the motor van. Operating costs were put at
£5,710 for the horses and £7,000 for the van. The figures came as a
revelation to many and the resultant pair of horses have been a much
admired special attraction ever since.

The other big question is whether or not we can continue to breed
them strong enough to work in a serious way. There is the whole future
of breeding and stock selection to think about, and no indication that
those in breed circles have done more than exploit a growing opportunity for trade; much as their fore-fathers did in the past to the
Clydesdale's detriment. Scientific minds have not been applied to any
problems in this field, and whilst one doubts that any intrusion would
be welcome there is a sneaking thought that very advanced methods
of breeding common to other stock could be applied advantageously.
It is time to computerize, and to think positively about steady improvement programmes.

It is now a century since Lord Arthur Cecil complained that the
typical English lorry horse lacked the right conformation. 'You could
knock together a better animal with a couple of battens and four posts'
he said, more in sadness than anger, and much to the discomfort of
Shire men. The fear is that the same sort of thing might be said of
Clydesdales in the future, due to the obvious fact that bloodlines are so
much more restricted and scarcity plus export demand are once more
resulting in the choicest breeding stock going away when they are
needed for home studs. Fortunately there tends to be acceptance of
return trade, but unsureness about whether environment cannot con-
fuse development.

The Horserace Betting Levy Board's financial help has benefited
heavy horses hugely, certainly making good any loss of government
aid. On the other hand there are many fewer good stallions kept and

quite a serious lack of knowledge on how even to handle them were numbers to increase. Stallion men were certainly born not made. 'Keep the lorry in view' will be remembered as the constant slogan and rallying call to Clydesdale breeders, but how can this be possible when it is success in the show ring which alone sets the standard? Weight and stamina for draught may be elusive if there are no lorries in sight and there may come a time when judges too must be given a basic training in order to influence higher standards of conformation and keep type up to scratch. Without their help we may well one day have the work without the horse-power and be even worse off.

Could there ever be a reversion to those early days of Drew and Riddell, with judicious crossing undertaken to infuse new blood? It is certainly a possibility, and might even become necessary if standards were allowed to fall. Even 20 years ago Hugh McGregor sold a stallion called Dunsyredene (23150) to James Prescott in the Manchester area, which was reputedly intended for crossing to Shire mares. Several other Clydesdales were apparently sent southwards for similar use. So the return traffic is a likely prospect, and no harm in it either if properly carried out through grading-up registers.

There is, too, another major dimension to the Clydesdale world which must be considered: it has an important role in the booming light horse business. Clydesdale influence in this respect is international and a hidden contribution which should really be given much more consideration. Sports such as show-jumping, horse trials, the hunting field, indeed wherever equines are in competition (including racing), owe some small part to heavy-horse foundation. Without the strength and substance of the like of the Clydesdale the Thoroughbreds and Arabs today would be breeding lightweights so lacking in endurance and wearing qualities as to be unsuited to competition. The percentage influence may be small in relation to the whole pedigree, but close examination on one side or the other will almost certainly reveal it is there. Often it comes in on the dam side and may be several generations back – and invariably is never acknowledged at all.

We can take precedents as far back as 1896, when the two best hunters in the country were by Clydesdale sires. There was another much-acclaimed hunter owned by the Duke of Portland, by a Thoroughbred horse out of a Clyde mare. More recently there was the outstanding point-to-point racehorse by the Clydesdale stallion Craigie Beau Ideal and out of an Irish T.B. mare, which also probably owed something to the heavy stock. There was that close challenger in the Grand National, Wyndburgh, three times second between 1957–62, and said to have a dash of Clyde in the make-up. Countless show champions could be listed, and almost every good show jumper or trials horse has had the benefit of the breeding line at some stage or other.

It seems a regrettable thing that credit is not given where it is due and all concerned would do well to take steps to correct such important omissions. It is in the interests of sport, because the more good lines of Clydesdales and other heavy horse breeds are fostered and encouraged, then the more assured we may be that there will be a reservoir of the right breeding influences upon which to draw for further generations of sound foundation stock. The Betting Levy Board's support is not wholly altruistic, even though many suppose it is sheer benevolence.

It is worth pointing out also that it is not only in bloodlines that the Clydesdale has benefited other equines, because there is no doubt at all that the knowledge its breeders possessed has been put to good account in other ways. McGregor, for example, turned to breeding Highland ponies with the quality of action he expected in Clydesdales, doing much in the passing to ensure a riding type. The Sleigh family, and Kerr of Harviestoun, turned their skills to improving native Shetland ponies, with the result that instead of well-rounded barrelled stock suited to the pits, we began to get gay little movers that were miniature horses and much in demand throughout the world. Now they are being driven and that lively action is much appreciated. Families like the Baillies and the Barries, involved with Clydesdales over many generations turned from them to greet the new sport of show-jumping with splendid enthusiasm, as proof that the instinct for the horse is bred into humans. In whatever form it emerged there has been major contribution to the equine progress and much enrichment to the sporting world in general.

With ample evidence of support in many differing areas then, there need be no doubt but that the future is assured. The trust that is passed on to successive generations will ensure that standards are made and kept, and even surpassed in the never-ending quest for improvement in type and performance. There will always be temptations and snares along the path, but there are challenges too, and every indication that they will not lack champions. The Clydesdale is a mighty horse, a rich part of our heritage, and its followers cast a mighty fine shadow themselves!

Fourteen

Clydesdale Crack

There is a most agreeable tradition in the Clydesdale world that wherever enthusiasts meet they'll lean over the wall or take a seat and have what is known as a crack or talk about the horses. Actually it is not so much a tradition as one of those inevitable happenings, for such is the enthusiasm and so genuine the interest that they cannot help it. Most are extremely knowledgeable too, being able to recite the antecedents of the majority of the leading horses past and present, knowing the way they bred and the awards that their stock won in the showyards.

It is simple indulgence and one that never wearies; moreover it is open to any who share this particular passion or love affair. Knowing this it seemed only right to finish a book about Clydesdales with just a crack about odds and ends of interest. So here we are ranging over all manner of happenings linked with the horses. Some may stir the memory and bring forth comparisons or draw conjecture, and most make some indirect comment about the characteristics of the Clydes and their followers.

Where to begin? Well, surely it is interesting and a footnote to courage that on one noted occasion a Clydesdale stallion fought with a bull. It was in Ohio and came about when the bull jumped a fence and promptly engaged the horse in combat. Seemingly there was a terrible struggle but after ten minutes the bull gored and inflicted a mortal wound on the Clydesdale, but not before it had been fearfully bitten and bruised.

A lawsuit worth recalling which was almost as celebrated at the time as Dunlop v Kilpatrick was that of Brown v Hunter in 1924 on grounds that the latter's stallion, Savrona (19554), would not get foals. Included in evidence was that Fyvie Baron when in Kintyre district had had the worst percentage of foals with only 12 per 100 mares. Since Savrona had been exported to Toronto the case was heard there and it was said in court that the horse would never draw (erect) for a mare but simply ate grass. Also that the groom fed the stallion Spanish fly, fenugreek, *Nuxvomica*, and ginger, plus four raw eggs three times a day for a month, and even then it wilted with the first mare. The pursuer won with expenses.

This sad story illustrates what was a major problem for stallion owners in the latter part of last century. It resulted of course from stallions being commercially exploited and being given 150 or 200 mares to cover in a season, when normally 80 was considered enough work. Great interest was shown in a 'Hewish impregnator' tried out at Glasgow Veterinary College by Professor M'Call. It was so·successful that a good many mares were sent to the Professor and it proved embarrassing!

By the way, there was once a court case brought between two Cumberland breeders for stallion service fees due for 20 years previously. The judge thought it most extraordinary that they had let matters stand over so long.

Accidental discoveries are legion. One worth recounting is of the veterinary surgeon Matthew M'Dougall who was sent out to castrate some colts. He so liked the looks of one that he left it entire – it proved to be the great stallion Sir Everard, cost £65 ... and bred Baron's Pride.

Now here's an odd story. An Angus farmer was working his horse in a potato crop when a queen bee went into its open mouth and the swarm followed, pouring down into the animal's stomach. It went quite berserk about the field, was badly damaged and finally succumbed totally.

Superstition and mystery are rife in the horse business. One idea that persisted is that the sire of a first covering would leave its influence on future progeny. So positive was this view that research was undertaken using zebras to try and trace the stripes through, but seemingly the issue was never resolved and convincing stories continued to be told affirming the idea. Was it linked with Shire usage?

One breeder was adamant that when he chose a horse with any white about it which he did not wish to be repeated in foals, he would never let the mare see the stallion's markings. She was blindfolded until service was completed and the horse removed. Then before taking the covers off he would insist on a horse being around of the colourings and markings he sought for the foal and was quite convinced that this worked.

There was an odd case in 1924 of a mare with an eye inflamed due to dust from the threshing mill; when she foaled three months later the foal was eyeless, or rather had eyes the size of peas. Her foal two years later was the same.

Another oddity in 1904 from Newcastle where two Clydesdale mares in foal were run down by a tramcar: both foaled healthy progeny and were again covered by the same stallion, but the following year they both had breach presentations and deformed foals – one lacked a near hind foot, and as it happened the dam had lost part of the same foot in the accident.

There are numerous reports of freak foals. One was born with two faces and three eyes; another with an extra foot. There have been instances of triplets and multiple twins – four mares bearing two foals each to the same stud horse. One strange case was of a mare producing a foal that resembled neither sire nor dam, but the pony on which the groom rode taking her to the stallion . . . and they swore it was a gelding!

Interesting stories relate to the wisdom of Clydesdales. There was a stallion called Royalist, said to have as much brain as his master (which of course could be true) but anyhow the groom after sounding his praises long and loudly over the brown ale set off home in glorious state. Subsequently he lay down in the roadway, leaving the horse to go on. Apparently he noticed his man's absence after a mile and went back. Finding him, the stallion neighed and whinnied and finally shook his jacket until he was aroused and grabbed Royalist's tail and hung on for two miles home.

Stallion leaders were always amazing characters and their arrival was quite an event in the farm household. There was at least one reputed to try to keep ahead of his horse in giving service.

Pay tribute to the grooms – they were great men. There was James MacDonald who travelled a horse in Moray and Nairn for 42 years. On retirement in 1905 he was given a purse of 61 sovereigns. Outstanding men in the '20s were John Coubray of Harviestoun, James Morgan of St John's Wells, Fleming of Craigie Mains, and McKnight who worked with the Montgomery stud, plus Sandy Caldwell who was Dunlop's man.

How splendid is the story of a Clydesdale breeder's reaction to a proposal from fellow breeders that as testimony to his skill they would have his portrait done in oils. Horrified he implored them on no account to have him done below the knees – because he felt he had not got the right Clydesdale kind of feet and no pastern.

They praised Saul Park of Manswraes too in his day, because in the mid-nineteenth century he bore losses with equanimity. When his horse Young Lofty, worth £1,000, died, he remarked to a consoling friend: 'Sir, it might have been a body's self that went as well.' He once won first prize with a Clydesdale stallion whose mother was a Highland pony.

There's an interesting story about J. P. Sleigh, who once missed his chance of buying a very superior champion horse – and the reason was that he was vexed with the breeder for calling a horse after his sister . . .

A Clydesdale was once made mascot of a Canadian curling team. It died after six months, so curlers from Fife sent another one.

Many an hour has been passed by Clydesdale men discussing the details of show preparation. When the hair and legs of Clydes for show were becoming a fetish they used soft soap and castor oil whipped to a paste on them, then put the legs into light boots to prevent tramping of the hair. One worthy commented in 1895 that they were using as much soap on the horses' legs as would run a laundry. So lengthy was hair then that it would often be plaited.

A solution that was advanced to the problem of teaching a horse its paces, was to take a piece of lead and fasten it to each leg above the ankle joint.

Could it have been true that when a Clydesdale was seen minus tail the owner explained that the horse's joints were so sharp and he went so close behind that they just could not keep a tail on him?

Query put forward in 1883: Will sewing a horse's ear tips help to prevent kicking? An expert judge thought it doubtful of success and besides a cruel practice.

There was once a court case that went through five hearings, and all over the question of the mare that had been sold and never lay down to rest and so was always unfit for work. But Professor W. Dick, of the famous Edinburgh veterinary college which bears his name, noted in 1844 that a Clydesdale drawing a 35cwt load of coal over four miles three times or 12 miles a day, was never known to lie down in eight years, except twice when sick.

The measurements of leading sires were often being quoted: Take these examples from 1891 when not in show condition: Prince of Albion (foaled 1886) 16.3 hands high on plates, 7ft 4in. in girth, 23½in. arm, 11½in. bone below knee, 12½in. below hock, 14½in. point of hock to fetlock; Sir Everard (foaled 1885) fully 17.1 hands high, 8ft girth (lean), weight 20¾cwt, arm 26in. upper muscle, knee 17in. round, 11in. bone below knee, 12in. below hock, point of hock to fetlock 18½in.

Last words go with the enthusiast who directed in his will that there was to be no funeral hearse, but instead a farm cart drawn by his two favourite Clydesdales.

Appendix A

CAWDOR CUP–WINNERS

Male	Female
1892 W. Renwick, Prince Alexander (8899)	J. Lockhart, Irene (12641)
1893 J. Kilpatrick, Prince of Kyle (7155)	J. Gilmour, Queen of the Roses (12302)
1894 P. Crawford, Prince of Carruchan (8151)	J. Gilmour, Moss Rose (6203)
1895 A. Dewar, Royal Gartly (9844)	J. Gilmour, Moss Rose (6203)
1886 A. Dewar, Royal Gartly (9844)	J. Martin, Montrave Maude (11786)
1897 P. Crawford, Prince of Carruchan (8151)	H. Webster, Lady Lothian (13319)
1898 M. Marshall, Hiawatha (10067)	J. Martin, Montrave Maude (11786)
1899 J. Pollock, Hiawatha (10067)	H. Webster, Lady Victoria (14582)
1900 No award	H. Webster, Lady Victoria (14582)
1901 J. Pollock, Hiawatha (10067)	H. Webster, Lady Victoria (14582)
1902 J. Pollock, Hiawatha (10067)	T. Smith, Royal Ruby (21619)
1903 M. Marshall, Marcellus (11110)	T. Smith, Cedric Princess (15274)
1904 G. Alston, Revelanta (11876)	A Guild, Lady Margaret (13833)
1905 M. Marshall, Hiawatha Godolphin (12662)	W. Park, Rosadora (16295)
1906 J. Kilpatrick, Oyama (13118)	W. Park, Pyrene (19757)
1907 M. Marshall, Baron Kitchener (10499)	T. Smith, Chester Princess (16371)
1908 M. Marshall, Memento (13100)	J. E. Kerr, Nerissa (30940)
1909 R. Brydon, Bonnie Buchlyvie (14032)	J. P. Sleigh, Moira (33747)
1910 W. Dunlop, Dunure Footprint (15203)	S. Mitchell, Boquhan Lady Peggy (33395)
1911 M. Marshall, Macaroni (15936)	J. E. Kerr, Harviestoun Cicely
1912 P. Sommerville, Scotland Yet (14839)	W. Ritchie, Harviestoun Baroness (27086)
1913 W. Dunlop, The Dunure (16839)	J. E. Kerr, Harviestoun Phyllis (37631)

1914   W. Dunlop, Dunure Refiner (17872)   W. Dunlop, Dunure Chosen

1915   J. Samson, Drumcross Radiant (18323)   A. Brooks Lady Betty

1916   W. Dunlop, Dunure Kaleidoscope (18335)   G. A. Ferguson, Rosalind

1917   J. P. Sleigh, Kismet (18417)   No contest

1918   J. Kilpatrick, Craigie Litigant (19071)   No contest

1919   G. A. Ferguson, Ardendale (18993)   J. P. Sleigh, Wells Lady Ray (44060)

1920   T. Clark, Rising Star (19836)   L. Wallace, Veda (48672)

1921   J. Kilpatrick, Craigie Excellence (19971)   W. Brown, Farleton Lady Alice (47512)

1922   A. M. Montgomery, Fyvie Sensation (20042)   J. P. Sleigh, Wells Mescal

1923   W. Moore Black, Flashdale (20576)   J. P. Sleigh, Raysun (56197)

1924   J. Kilpatrick, Craigie M'Quaid (20724)   J. Kilpatrick, Craigie Ella (56917)

1925   J. Kilpatrick, Craigie Exquisite (21053)   T. & M. Templeton, Monk Gladys (56232)

1926   T. & M. Templeton, Benefactor (20867)   A. Murdoch, Orange Blossom (57427)

1927   R. Park, Brunstane Again (20717)   R. Park, Brunstane Phyllis (57786)

1928   D. Adam, Satisfaction (21293)   A. Murdoch, Mary Rose

1929   J. Kilpatrick, Craigie Winalot (21322)   A. Murdoch, Fyvie Primrose

1930   J. Kilpatrick, Craigie Beau Ideal (21856)   J. E. Kerr, Harviestoun Alanna (58072)

1931   J. Johnston & Son, Dunmore Supreme (21753)   A. Murdoch, Onoway

1932   T. & M. Templeton, Beneficial   G. M. Beck, Lane Lucky Girl

1933   J. Kilpatrick, Craigie Realisation   A. Murdoch, Faraway

1934   T. & M. Templeton, Watchword (22355)   Lord Dalziel, Charm O'Borgue

1935   J. Kilpatrick, Craigie Magnificent   D. Adams, Powerful Link

1936   J. Clark, Windlaw Aristocrat   A. Murdoch, Rosetta

1937   A. Clark, Strathore Imperial   J. M'Farlane, Mary

1938   G. & J. Campbell's colt   A. Murdoch, Titania

1939   J. Kilpatrick, Craigie Independent (23511)   J. M'Farlane, Myrene

1940   No contest   No contest

1941   J. Kilpatrick, Craigie Topsman   No contest

1942   J. Kilpatrick, Craigie Chieftain (23338)   No contest

1943   T. Clark & Son, Muirton Monarch (23787)   No contest

1944   H. Murdoch & Son, Balgreen Final Command (24094)   W. & J. Kean, Chapelton Colleen (68304)

1945 J. Barr, Union Jack (24076) — J. M'Farlane, Gleneagles Helena

1946 Jas. Kilpatrick, Hawkrigg Headline (23887) — D. & D. N. Blair, Littleinch Morag (66431)

1947 J. Kilpatrick, Craigie Supreme Commander (24123) — G. M. Beck, Brougham Real (70835)

1948 J. Kilpatrick, Craigie True Form (24449) — A. Sommerville, Cowden Primula

1949 T. Clark & Son, Regal Monarch (24474) — J. M'Farlane, Gleneagles Hilda

1950 J. Kilpatrick, Craigie Commodore (24514) — W. Craig, Dryburgh Priscilla

1951 T. Clark & Son, Muirton Sensation — J. A. Armstrong, Tarraby Mirabeau

1952 J. Barr, Dunsyre Footprint (24610) — R. Donald, Ballochmorris Mist

1953 A. Kilpatrick, Craigie Superb — J. McFarlane & Sons, Gleneagles Blossom

1954 J. Tennant, Gleneagles Diplomat — J. Kirkwood & Sons, Dockenflat Linda

1955 T. Clark & Son, Muirton Supreme — Ibbett & McKenzie, Princess Charming

1956 A. Sleigh, Tolquhoun Windsor — J. Barrie, Howford Classic Lady

1957 A. Kilpatrick, Craigie Starlight — R. Mitchell, Sensation

1958 A. Kilpatrick, Craigie Leader — Brown Bros., Glororum Patricia

1959 J. Thomson's colt — J. G. Glashen, Milltimber Snowflake

1960 A. Kilpatrick, Craigie Paramount — A. Hardie, Westerton Rose Marie

1961 A. Kilpatrick, Craigie Gallant Hero — J. Chapman, Heather Perfection

1962 T. Clark & Son, Muirton Security — H. & A. Hall, Glasserton Winsome

1963 R. Mitchell, Magnificent — G. Brown, Glororum Petula

1964 J. C. Picken, Torrs Renown — Messrs. Brown, Glororum Valentia

1965 J. W. Young & Son, Doura Ambassador — F. P. Kennedy & Son, Blackhall Cherry Blossom

1966 J. Chapman, Johnston Realisation — J. Chapman, Heather Enchantress

1967 J. W. Young & Son, Doura Excelsior — G. Brown, Glororum Maria

1968 J. Chapman, Johnston Leader — J. Chapman, Heather Enchantress

1969 J. Brewster & Son, Bandirran Benefactor — D. W. McNaught, Queen of Carrick

1970 J. W. Young & Son, Doura Aristocrat — A. Hardie & Son, Westerton Princess

1971 J. Sommerville, Smeaton Perfection — H. Black, Collessie Lady Arden

1972 J. W. Young & Son, Doura Majestic — J. W. Young & Son, Doura Sweet Melody

1973 P. Sharp, Bardrill Enterprise — J. Clark, Windlaw Svetlana

1974 J. W. Young & Son, Doura Mandate — J. Brewster & Son, Bandirran Beau Belle

1975 J. W. Young & Son, Doura Everlasting — Q. McMorland, Queen of the Roses

1976 J. W. Young & Son, Doura Masterstroke — W. Murdoch & Sons, Balgreen Baroness

1977 James W. Young, Greendykes Excelsior Again — R. Lawrie, Kettlestoun Lucinda

1978 J. W. Young & Son, Doura Stepping Stone — W. Murdoch & Sons, Balgreen Silver Lining

1979 H. & W. Ramsay, Millisle Print — W. Murdoch & Sons, Balgreen Lady Linda

Appendix B

CHAMPION STALLIONS (1836 to 1892)

1836 A. Galbraith, Stirlingshire
Champion (830)
no records until
1854 S. Clark, Lofty (455)
1855 P. Crawford, Lord Raglan (492)
1856 J. Young, Lofty (457)
1857 C. Philips, Merry Tom (532)
1859 P. Crawford, Lofty Ben
Lomond (468)
1861 D. Riddell
1862 D. Riddell, Sir Walter Scott
1863 W. Kerr
1864 J. & W. Muir, Lofty 3rd (469)
1865 J. Kerr
1866 S. Clark, Young Lofty (987)
1867 S. Clark, Young Lofty (987)
1868 D. Riddell, Young Campsie
1869 D. Riddell, Young Campsie
1870 J. Kerr, Conqueror (196)
1871 J. Kerr, Conqueror (196)
1872 R. M'Kean, Premier (595)
1873 P. Crawford, Crown Prince (206)
1874 D. Riddell, Time O'Day (875)
1875 D. Riddell, Time O'Day (875)
1876 D. Riddell, Darnley (222)

1877 D. Riddell, Darnley (222)
1878 P. Crawford, Strathclyde (1538)
1879 D. Riddell, Bonny Breastknot
(108)
1880 J. McNab, Champion of the
North (1092)
1881 A. M'Kay, Hawkhead
1882 D. Riddell, St. Lawrence (3220)
1883 D. Riddell, St. Lawrence (3220)
1884 L. Drew, Prince of Avondale
1885 J. Pollock, Gallant Lad (2781)
1886 J. M'Donald, Lord Hopetoun
(2965)
1887 J. Waddell, Young Duke of
Hamilton
1888 J. Kilpatrick, Knight of
Ellerslie (3737)
1889 W. Taylor, Sir Everard (5353)
1890 W. Taylor, Sir Everard (5353)
1891 J. Pollock, Flashwood (3604)
1892 D. Riddell, Moneycorn

(Every effort has been made to produce
accurate lists of champions and any errors
are regretted.)

Appendix C

CLYDESDALE STUD BOOK SOCIETY PRESIDENTS

1877–78 The Earl of Dunmore	1920–21 R. Park
1878–80 The Earl of Dunmore	1921–22 George A. Ferguson
1880–81 The Earl of Strathmore	1923–24 A. M. Montgomery
1881–82 Lord Arthur Cecil	1924–25 W. W. Philip
1882–83 Sir Michael Shaw-Stewart	1925–26 J. P. Sleigh
1883–84 The Earl of Galloway	1926–27 Robt. Lumsden
1884–85 The Duke of Montrose	1927–29 Wm. Meiklem
1885–86 The Earl of Aberdeen	1929–31 James Picken
1886–87 The Duke of Portland	1931–33 Thomas Clark
1887–88 John Gilmore	1933–35 G. A. Marshall
1888–89 The Earl of Hopetoun	1935–36 Wm. Brown
1889–90 The Duke of Fife	1936–37 Wm. Brown
1890–91 Lord Polwarth	1937–39 G. Findlater
1891–93 The Earl of Cawdor	1939–42 J. Ernest Kerr
1893–95 The Marquis of Londonderry	1942–44 Prof. J. R. McCall
1895–96 The Duke of Buccleuch	1944–45 Jas. Kilpatrick
1896–97 Sir R. D. Moncrieffe	1945–46 Jas. Kilpatrick
1897– Sir J. Gilmore then	1946–47 Alex Murdoch
1900 Principal M'Call	1947–49 John Kerr
1900–01 J. Douglas Fletcher	1949–51 A. Gilmore
1901–02 J. Douglas Fletcher	1951–53 J. C. Drennan
1902–03 St. Clair Cunningham	1953–55 Matt. Templeton
1903–05 Robert Brydon	1955–57 Alex. Sleigh
1905–06 Sir J. Stirling Maxwell	1957–59 A. Kilpatrick
1906–08 Sir J. Stirling Maxwell	1959–62 A. Sommerville
1908–09 J. Ernest Kerr	1962–64 G. Brown
1909–11 H. B. Marshall	1964–66 J. G. Glashan
1911–12 Stephen Mitchell	1966–68 Hugh Black
1912–13 Stephen Mitchell	1968–70 J. Brewster
1913–15 Jas. Boyd	1970–72 J. Clark
1915–16 George Bean	1972–74 Wm. Bankier
1916–18 J. Ernest Kerr	1974–76 J. McNicol
1918–19 Wm. Montgomery	1976–78 Wm. Murdoch
1919–20 Jas. Kilpatrick	1978–80 J. Picken

Bibliography

For this work the author has consulted a lengthy list of references, with the largest contribution from volumes of the *North British Agriculturist, Farming News* and the *Scottish Farmer* weekly and annual numbers. In addition the following works have been consulted, with special reference to the first named sources:

Clydesdale Stud Books, particularly the retrospective volume, 1878 onwards
My Seventy Years with Clydesdales, J. Kilpatrick Memoirs (Munro, Perth 1949)
Highland Society Transactions, early volumes
Journals of Royal Agricultural Society of England, early volumes
The Horse, J. H. Walsh (London 1862)
The British Farmer's Cyclopedia of Improved Modern Husbandry, T. W. S. Potts
    (2nd edit., London 1808)
Medieval History, Stephenson (London 1962)
History of Horse Breeds, D. M. Goodall (Hale, London 1977)
The Shire Horse, K. Chivers (Allan, London 1976)
Heavy Horses, H. Biddell and others (Vinton, London 1905)
Book of the Horse, Sidney – as quoted (Cassell, London)
The Cavalry, J. Lawford, edit. (Sampson Low, London 1976)
Elements of Agriculture, W. Fream, edit. (Murray, London 1972, 15th edition)
Works of Robert Burns (Paterson edit. 1879)
Heavy Horses, past and present, E. Hart (David & Charles, Devon 1976)
English Horse-drawn Vehicles, D. Parry (Warne, London 1979)

Index

Names of horses in *italics*